DON'T WASTE YOUR LIFE

DON'T WASTE YOUR LIFE

John Piper

CROSSWAY BOOKS
WHEATON, ILLINOIS

Don't Waste Your Life (Group Study Edition)

Copyright © 2007 by Desiring God Foundation

Text updated 2009

Published by Crossway Books
        a publishing ministry of Good News Publishers
        1300 Crescent Street
        Wheaton, Illinois 60187

This Group Study Edition is based on and is a companion to
Don't Waste Your Life by John Piper (Crossway Books, 2003).

Italics in biblical quotes indicate emphasis added.

Scripture quotations are taken from the ESV® Bible (*The Holy Bible, English Standard Version®*). Copyright © 2001 by Crossway Bibles, a publishing ministry of Good News Publishers. Used by permission. All rights reserved.

Other Scripture quotations are from:

The Holy Bible, New International Version (NIV). © 1973, 1978, 1984 by International Bible Society. Used by permission of Zondervan Publishing House. All rights reserved.

The Holy Bible, King James Version (KJV)

Cover design: Matt Taylor, Taylor Design Works

Cover photo: Getty Images

First printing, redesign 2009

Printed in the United States of America

ISBN 13: 978-1-4335-0632-1

ISBN 10: 1-4335-0632-7

Library of Congress Cataloging-in-Publication Data
Piper, John, 1946-
    Don't waste your life / John Piper.
      p. cm.
    Includes bibliographical references.
    ISBN 13: 978-1-58134-498-1 (pbk. : alk. paper)
    ISBN 10: 1-58134-498-8
    1. Christian life. I. Title
BV4501.3.P555   2003
248.4—dc21   2003007833

ML		19	18	17	16	15	14	13	12	11	10
13	12	11	10	9	8	7	6	5	4	3	2

To
Louie Giglio
and the passion of his heart
for the renown of Jesus Christ
in this generation

CONTENTS

PREFACE

For Christians and Non-Christians

The Bible says, "You are not your own, for you were bought with a price. So glorify God in your body" (1 Corinthians 6:19-20). I have written this book to help you taste those words as sweet instead of bitter or boring.

You are in one of two groups: Either you are a Christian, or God is now calling you to be one. You would not have picked up this book if God were not at work in your life.

If you are a Christian, you are not your own. Christ has bought you at the price of his own death. You now belong doubly to God: He made you, and he bought you. That means your life is not your own. It is God's. Therefore, the Bible says, "Glorify God in your body." God made you for this. He bought you for this. This is the meaning of your life.

If you are not yet a Christian, that is what Jesus Christ offers: doubly belonging to God, and being able to do what you were made for. That may not sound exciting. Glorifying God may mean nothing to you. That's why I tell my story in the first two chapters, called "Created for Joy." It was not always plain to me that pursuing God's glory would be virtually the same as pursing my joy. Now I see that millions of people waste their lives because they think these paths are two and not one.

There is a warning. The path of God-exalting joy will cost you your life. Jesus said, "Whoever loses his life for my sake and the gospel's will save it." In other words, it is better to lose your life than to waste it. If you live gladly to make others glad in God, your life will be hard, your risks will be high, and your joy will be full. This is not a book about how to avoid a wounded life, but how to avoid a *wasted* life. Some of you will die in the service of Christ. That will not be a tragedy. Treasuring life above Christ is a tragedy.

Please know that I am praying for you, whether you are a student dreaming something radical for your life, or whether you are retired and hoping not to waste the final years. If you wonder what I am praying, read Chapter 10. That is my prayer.

For now, I thank God for you. My joy grows with every soul that seeks the glory of God in the face of Jesus Christ. Remember, you have one life. That's all. You were made for God. Don't waste it.

March 31, 2003
John Piper

CHAPTER 1

MY SEARCH FOR A SINGLE PASSION TO LIVE BY

My father was an evangelist. When I was a boy, there were rare occasions when my mother and sister and I traveled with him and heard him preach. I trembled to hear my father preach. In spite of the predictable opening humor, the whole thing struck me as absolutely blood-earnest. There was a certain squint to his eye and a tightening of his lips when the avalanche of biblical texts came to a climax in application.

"I'VE WASTED IT, I'VE WASTED IT"

Oh, how he would plead! Children, teenagers, young singles, young married people, the middle-aged, old people—he would press the warnings and the wooings of Christ into the heart of each person. He had stories, so many stories, for each age group—stories of glorious conversions, and stories of horrific refusals to believe followed by tragic deaths. Seldom could those stories come without tears.

For me as a boy, one of the most gripping illustrations my fiery father used was the story of a man converted in old age.

The church had prayed for this man for decades. He was hard and resistant. But this time, for some reason, he showed up when my father was preaching. At the end of the service, during a hymn, to everyone's amazement he came and took my father's hand. They sat down together on the front pew of the church as the people were dismissed. God opened his heart to the Gospel of Christ, and he was saved from his sins and given eternal life. But that did not stop him from sobbing and saying, as the tears ran down his wrinkled face—and what an impact it made on me to hear my father say this through his own tears—"I've wasted it! I've wasted it!"

This was the story that gripped me more than all the stories of young people who died in car wrecks before they were converted—the story of an old man weeping that he had wasted his life. In those early years God awakened in me a fear and a passion not to waste my life. The thought of coming to my old age and saying through tears, "I've wasted it! I've wasted it!" was a fearful and horrible thought to me.

"ONLY ONE LIFE, 'TWILL SOON BE PAST"

Another riveting force in my young life—small at first, but oh so powerful over time—was a plaque that hung in our kitchen over the sink. We moved into that house when I was six. So I suppose I looked at the words on that plaque almost every day for twelve years, till I went away to college at age eighteen. It was a simple piece of glass painted black on the back with a gray link chain snug around it for a border and for hanging. On the front, in old English script, painted in white, were the words:

Only one life,
'Twill soon be past;
Only what's done
for Christ will last.

To the left, beside these words, was a painted green hill with two trees and a brown path that disappeared over the hill. How many times, as a little boy, and then as a teenager with pimples and longings and anxieties, I looked at that brown path (my life) and wondered what would be over that hill. The message was clear. You get one pass at life. That's all. Only one. And the lasting measure of that life is Jesus Christ. That very plaque hung on the wall by our front door for years. I saw it every time I left home.

What would it mean to waste my life? That was a burning question. Or, more positively, what would it mean to live well— not to waste life, but to . . . ? How to finish that sentence was *the* question. I was not even sure how to put the question into words, let alone what the answer might be. What was the opposite of not wasting my life? "To be successful in a career"? Or "to be maximally happy"? Or "to accomplish something great?" Or "to find the deepest meaning and significance"? Or "to help as many people as possible"? Or "to serve Christ to the full"? Or "to glorify God in all I do"? Or was there a point, a purpose, a focus, an essence to life that would fulfill every one of those dreams?

"THE LOST YEARS"

I had forgotten how weighty this question was for me until I looked through my files from those early years. Just when I was about to leave my South Carolina home in 1964, never to return as a resident, Wade Hampton High School published a simple literary magazine of poems and stories. Near the back, with the byline Johnny Piper, was a poem. I will spare you. It was not a good poem. Jane, the editor, was merciful. What matters to me now was the title and first four lines. It was called "The Lost Years." Beside it was a sketch of an old man in a rocking chair. The poem began:

Long I sought for the earth's hidden meaning;
Long as a youth was my search in vain.
Now as I approach my last years waning,
My search I must begin again.

Across the fifty years that separate me from that poem I can hear the fearful refrain, "I've wasted it! I've wasted it!" Somehow there had been wakened in me a passion for the essence and the main point of life. The ethical question "whether something is permissible" faded in relation to the question, "what is the main thing, the essential thing?" The thought of building a life around minimal morality or minimal significance—a life defined by the question, "What is permissible?"—felt almost disgusting to me. I didn't want a minimal life. I didn't want to live on the outskirts of reality. I wanted to understand the main thing about life and pursue it.

EXISTENTIALISM WAS THE AIR WE BREATHED

The passion not to miss the *essence* of life, not to waste it, intensified in college—the tumultuous late sixties. There were strong reasons for this, reasons that go well beyond the inner turmoil of one boy coming of age. "Essence" was under assault almost everywhere. Existentialism was the air we breathed. And the meaning of existentialism was that "existence precedes essence." That is, first you exist and then, by existing, you create your essence. You make your essence by freely choosing to be what you will be. There is no essence outside you to pursue or conform to. Call it "God" or "Meaning" or "Purpose"—it is not there until you create it by your own courageous existence. (If you furrow your brow and think, "This sounds strangely like our own day and what we call postmodernism," don't be surprised. There is nothing new under the sun. There are only endless repackagings.)

I recall sitting in a darkened theater watching the theatrical offspring of existentialism, the "theater of the absurd." The play was Samuel Beckett's *Waiting for Godot*. Vladimir and Estragon meet under a tree and converse as they wait for Godot. He never comes. Near the end of the play a boy tells them Godot will not be coming. They decide to leave but never move. They go nowhere. The curtain falls, and God[ot] never comes.

That was Beckett's view of people like me—waiting, seeking, hoping to find the *Essence* of things, instead of creating my own essence with my free and unbridled existence. Nowhere—that's where you're going, he implied, if you pursue some transcendent Point or Purpose or Focus or Essence.

"THE NOWHERE MAN"

The Beatles released their album *Rubber Soul* in December 1965 and sang out their existentialism with compelling power for my generation. Perhaps it was clearest in John Lennon's "Nowhere Man."

> *He's a real nowhere man*
> *Sitting in his nowhere land*
> *Making all his nowhere plans*
> *For nobody*
> *Doesn't have a point of view*
> *Knows not where he's going to*
> *Isn't he a bit like you and me?*

These were heady days, especially for college students. And, thankfully, God was not silent. Not everybody gave way to the lure of the absurd and the enticement of heroic emptiness. Not everyone caved in to the summons of Albert Camus and Jean-Paul Sartre. Even voices without root in the Truth knew that there must be something more—something outside ourselves, something bigger and greater and more worth living for than what we saw in the mirror.

THE ANSWER, THE ANSWER WAS BLOWIN' IN THE WIND

Bob Dylan was scratching out songs with oblique messages of hope that exploded on the scene precisely because they hinted at a Reality that would not keep us waiting forever. Things would change. Sooner or later the slow would be fast and the first would be last. And it would not be because we were existential masters of our absurd fate. It would come to us. That is what we all felt in the song, "The Times They Are A-Changin'."

The line it is drawn,
The curse it is cast,
The slow one now
Will later be fast.
As the present now
Will later be past,
The order is
Rapidly fadin'.
And the first one now
Will later be last,
For the times they are a-changin'.

It must have riled the existentialists to hear Dylan, perhaps without even knowing it, sweep away their everything-goes relativism with the audacious double "*The* answer . . . *The* answer" in the smash hit, "Blowin' in the Wind."

How many times must a man look up
Before he can see the sky?
Yes, 'n' how many ears must
  one man have

Before he can hear people cry?
Yes, 'n' how many deaths will it take
till he knows
That too many people have died?
The answer, my friend,
is blowin' in the wind,
The answer is blowin' in the wind.

How many times can a man look up and not see the sky? There is a sky up there to be seen. You may look up ten thousand times and say you don't see it. But that has absolutely no effect on its objective existence. It is there. And one day you will see it. How many times must you look up before you see it? There is an answer. *The* answer, *The* answer, my friend, is not yours to invent or create. It will be decided for you. It is outside you. It is real and objective and firm. One day you will hear it. You don't create it. You don't define it. It comes to you, and sooner or later you conform to it—or bow to it.

That is what I heard in Dylan's song, and everything in me said, Yes! There is an Answer with a capital A. To miss it would mean a wasted life. To find it would mean having a unifying Answer to all my questions.

The little brown path over the green hill on our kitchen plaque was winding its way—all through the sixties—among the sweet snares of intellectual folly. Oh, how courageous my generation seemed when they stepped off the path and put their foot in the trap! Some could even muster the moxie to boast, "I have chosen the way of freedom. I have created my own existence. I have shaken loose the old laws. Look how my leg is severed!"

THE MAN WITH LONG HAIR AND KNICKERS

But God was graciously posting compelling warnings along the way. In the fall of 1965 Francis Schaeffer delivered a week of lectures at Wheaton College that in 1968 became the book, *The God Who Is There*.[1] The title shows the stunning simplicity of the thesis. God is there. Not *in here*, defined and shaped by my own desires. God is *out there*. Objective. Absolute Reality (which Schaeffer pronounced something like "Reawity"). All that looks like reality to us is dependent on God. There is creation and Creator, nothing more. And creation gets all its meaning and purpose from God.

Here was an absolutely compelling road sign. Stay on the road of objective truth. This will be the way to avoid wasting your life. Stay on the road that your fiery evangelist father was on. Don't forsake the plaque on your kitchen wall. Here was weighty intellectual confirmation that life would be wasted in the grasslands of existentialism. Stay on the road. There is Truth. There is a Point and Purpose and Essence to it all. Keep searching. You will find it.

I suppose there is no point lamenting that one must spend his college years learning the obvious—that there is Truth, that there is objective being and objective value. Like a fish going to school to learn that there is water, or a bird that there is air, or a worm that there is dirt. But it seems that, for the last two hundred years or so, this has been the main point of good education. And its opposite is the essence of bad education. So I don't lament the years I spent learning the obvious.

THE MAN WHO TAUGHT ME TO SEE

Indeed, I thank God for professors and writers who devoted tremendous creative energies to render credible the existence of trees and water and souls and love and God. C. S. Lewis, who died the same day as John F. Kennedy in 1963 and who taught English at Oxford, walked up over the horizon of my little brown path in 1964 with such blazing brightness that it is hard to overstate the impact he had on my life.

Someone introduced me to Lewis my freshman year with the book, *Mere Christianity*.[2] For the next five or six years I was almost never without a Lewis book near at hand. I think that without his influence I would not have lived my life with as much joy or usefulness as I have. There are reasons for this.

He has made me wary of chronological snobbery. That is, he showed me that newness is no virtue and oldness is no vice. Truth and beauty and goodness are not determined by when they exist. Nothing is inferior for being old, and nothing is valuable for being modern. This has freed me from the tyranny of novelty and opened for me the wisdom of the ages. To this day I get most of my soul-food from centuries ago. I thank God for Lewis's compelling demonstration of the obvious.

He demonstrated for me and convinced me that rigorous, precise, penetrating logic is not opposed to deep, soul-stirring feeling and vivid, lively—even playful—imagination. He was a "romantic rationalist." He combined things that almost everybody today assumes are mutually exclusive: rationalism and poetry, cool logic and warm feeling, disciplined prose and free imagination. In shattering these old stereotypes, he freed me to think hard and to write poetry, to argue for the resurrection and compose hymns to Christ, to smash an argument and hug a friend, to demand a definition and use a metaphor.

Lewis gave me an intense sense of the "realness" of things. The preciousness of this is hard to communicate. To wake up in the morning and be aware of the firmness of the mattress, the warmth of the sun's rays, the sound of the clock ticking, the sheer being of things ("quiddity" as he calls it[3]). He helped me become alive to life. He helped me see what is there in the world—things that, if we didn't have, we would pay a million dollars to have, but having them, ignore. He made me more alive to beauty. He put my soul on notice that there are daily wonders that will waken worship if I open my eyes. He shook my dozing soul and threw the cold water of reality in my face, so that life and God and heaven and hell broke into my world with glory and horror.

He exposed the sophisticated intellectual opposition to objective being and objective value for the naked folly that it was. The philosophical king of my generation had no clothes on, and the writer of children's books from Oxford had the courage to say so.

> You can't go on "seeing through" things forever. The whole point of seeing through something is to see something through it. It is good that the window should be transparent, because the street or garden beyond it is opaque. How if you saw through the garden too? It is no use trying to "see through" first principles. If you see through everything, then everything is transparent. But a wholly transparent world is an invisible world. To "see through" all things is the same as not to see.[4]

Oh, how much more could be said about the world as C. S. Lewis saw it and the way he spoke. He has his flaws, some of them serious. But I will never cease to thank God for this remarkable man who came onto my path at the perfect moment.

A FIANCÉE IS A STUBBORNLY OBJECTIVE FACT

There was another force that solidified my unwavering belief in the unbending existence of objective reality. Her name was Noël Henry. I fell in love with her in the summer of 1966. Way too soon probably. But it has turned out okay; I still love her. Nothing sobers a wandering philosophical imagination like the thought of having a wife and children to support.

We were married in December 1968. It is a good thing to do one's thinking in relation to real people. From that moment on, every thought has been a thought in relationship. Nothing is merely an idea, but an idea that bears on my wife, then later, on my five children and an increasing number of grandchildren. I thank God for the parable of Christ and the church that I have been obliged to live these forty years. There are lessons in life—the unwasted life—that I would probably never have learned without this relationship (just as there are lessons in lifelong singleness that will probably be learned no other way).

I BLESS YOU, MONO, FOR MY LIFE

In the fall of 1966 God was closing in with an ever narrowing path for my life. When he made his next decisive move, Noël wondered where I had gone. The fall semester had started, and I did not show up in classes or in chapel. Finally she found me, flat on my back with mononucleosis in the health center, where I lay for three weeks. The life plan that I was so sure of four months earlier unraveled in my fevered hands.

In May I had felt a joyful confidence that my life would be most useful as a medical doctor. I loved biology; I loved the idea of healing people. I loved knowing, at last, what I was doing in college. So I quickly took general chemistry in summer school so I could catch up and take organic chemistry that fall.

Now with mono, I had missed three weeks of organic chemistry. There was no catching up. But even more important, Harold John Ockenga, then pastor of Park Street Church in Boston, was preaching in chapel each morning during the spiritual emphasis week. I was listening on WETN, the college radio station. Never had I heard exposition of the Scriptures like this. Suddenly all the glorious objectivity of Reality centered for me on the Word of God. I lay there feeling as if I had awakened from a dream, and knew, now that I was awake, what I was to do.

Noël came to visit, and I said, "What would you think if I didn't pursue a medical career but instead went to seminary?"

As with every other time I've asked that kind of question through the years, the answer was, "If that's where God leads you, that's where I'll go." From that moment on I have never doubted that my calling in life is to be a minister of the Word of God.

NOTES

1   Schaeffer's prophetic work remains incredibly relevant to our age. I'd encourage every one of my readers to read at least one work by Schaeffer. A good place to begin with the "best of the best" is *The Francis A. Schaeffer Trilogy: The God Who Is There, Escape from Reason, and He Is There and He Is Not Silent* (Wheaton, Ill.: Crossway Books, 1990).

2   C. S. Lewis, *Mere Christianity* (New York: Macmillan, 1952).

3   C. S. Lewis, *Surprised by Joy* (New York: Harcourt, Brace and World, 1955), 199.

4   C. S. Lewis, *The Abolition of Man* (New York: Macmillan, 1947), 91.

CHAPTER 2

BREAKTHROUGH—THE BEAUTY OF CHRIST, MY JOY

In 1968 I had no idea what it would mean for me to be a minister of the Word. Being a pastor was as far from my expectations as being a pastor's wife was from Noël's. What then? Would it mean being a teacher, a missionary, a writer, maybe a professor of literature with good theology? All I knew was that ultimate Reality had suddenly centered for me on the Word of God. The great Point and Purpose and Essence that I longed to link up with was now connected unbreakably with the Bible. The mandate was clear: "Do your best to present yourself to God as one approved, a worker who has no need to be ashamed, *rightly handling the word of truth*" (2 Timothy 2:15). For me, that meant seminary, with a focus on understanding and rightly handling the Bible.

LEARNING NOT TO CUT OFF MY OWN HEAD

The battle to learn the obvious continued. The modern assault on reality—that there exists a real objective reality outside ourselves that can be truly known—had turned Bible study into a swamp of subjectivity. You could see it in the church as small groups shared their subjective impressions about what Bible texts meant "for me" without an anchor in any original meaning. And you could see it in academic books as creative scholars cut their own heads off by arguing that texts have no objective meaning.

If there is only one life to live in this world, and if it is not to be wasted, nothing seemed more important to me than finding out what God really meant in the Bible, since he inspired men to write it. If that was up for grabs, then no one could tell which life is worthy and which life is wasted. I was stunned at the gamesmanship in the scholarly world as authors used all their intellectual powers to nullify what they themselves wrote! That is, they expressed theories of meaning that argued there is no single, valid meaning in texts. Ordinary people reading this book will (I hope) find this incredible. I don't blame you. It is. But the fact remains that to this day well-paid, well-fed professors use tuition and tax dollars to argue that "since literature does not accurately convey reality, literary interpretation need not accurately convey the reality which is literature."[1]

In other words, since we can't know objective reality outside ourselves, there can be no objective meaning in what we write either. So interpretation does not mean trying to find any objective thing that an author put in a text, but simply means that we express the ideas that enter our head as we read. Which doesn't really matter because when others read what we have written, they won't have any access to our intention either. It's all a game. Only it is sinister, because all these scholars (and small-group members) insist that their own love letters and contracts be measured by one rule: what they intended to say. Any mumbo-jumbo about creatively hearing "yes" when I wrote "no" will not go down at the bank or the marriage counselor.

And so it was that Existentialism came home to roost in the

Bible: Existence precedes essence. That is, I don't *find* meaning—I *create* it. The Bible is a lump of clay, and I am the potter. Interpretation is creation. My existence as a subject creates the "essence" of the object. Don't laugh. They were serious. They still are. Today it just has other names.

DEFENDING THE BRIGHTNESS OF THE BROAD-DAY SUN

Into this morass of subjectivity came a Professor of Literature from the University of Virginia, E. D. Hirsch. Reading his book *Validity in Interpretation* during my seminary years was like suddenly finding a rock under my feet in the quicksand of contemporary concepts about meaning. Like most of the guides God sent along my path, Hirsch defended the obvious. Yes, he argued, there *does* exist an original meaning that a writer had in his mind when he wrote. And yes, valid interpretation seeks that intention in the text and gives good reasons for claiming to see it. This seemed as obvious to me as the broad-day sun. It was everybody's assumption in daily life when they spoke or wrote.

Perhaps even more important, it seemed courteous. None of us wants our notes and letters and contracts interpreted differently than we intend them. Therefore, common courtesy, or the Golden Rule, requires that we read others the way we would be read. It seemed to me that much philosophical talk about meaning was just plain hypocritical: At the university I undermine objective meaning, but at home (and at the bank) I insist on it. I wanted no part of that game. It looked like an utterly wasted life. If there is no valid interpretation based on real objective, unchanging, original meaning, then my whole being said, "Let us eat, drink, and be merry. But by no means let us treat scholarship as if it really matters."

THE DEATH OF GOD AND THE DEATH OF MEANING

Things were coming together. On a cool April afternoon back in 1966 at Wheaton College I had taken the new *Time* Magazine to a second-floor corner of the library and read the cover story: "Is God Dead?" (April 8, 1966). "Christian atheists" like Thomas J. J. Altizer answered, yes. It was not new news. Friedrich Nietzsche had given the obituary a hundred years earlier: "Whither is God? . . . I will tell you. We have killed him—you and I. All of us are his murderers. . . . God is dead. God remains dead and we have killed him."[2] It was a costly confession: Nietzsche spent the last eleven years of his life in a semi-catatonic state and died in 1900.

But the courageous "Christian atheists" of the sixties did not compute the costs of being God's replacement as supermen (which Nietzsche called them). The strong drink of Existentialism loosened the tongues of those creative theologians, like the men five rows back in the airplane after too many beers. So the suicidal assertion that God is dead was spoken again. And when God died, the meaning of texts died. If the basis of objective reality dies, then writing and speaking about objective reality die. It all hangs together.

So my deliverance in the late sixties from the madness of killing God led naturally in the early seventies to my deliverance from the hypocritical emptiness of hermeneutical subjectivism—the two-faced notion that there is no objective meaning in any sentence (but this one). Now I was ready for the real work of seminary: finding what the Bible said about how not to waste my life.

LEARNING THE "SEVERE DISCIPLINE" OF READING THE BIBLE

My debt at this point to Daniel Fuller is incalculable. He taught hermeneutics—the science of how to interpret the Bible. Not only did he introduce me to E. D. Hirsch and force me to read him with rigor, but he also taught me how to read the Bible with what Matthew Arnold called "severe discipline." He showed me the obvious: that the verses of the Bible are not strung pearls but links in a chain. The writers developed unified patterns of thought. They reasoned. "Come now, let us reason together, says the LORD" (Isaiah 1:18). This meant that, in each paragraph of Scripture, one should ask how each part related to the other parts in order to say one coherent thing. Then the paragraphs should be related to each other in the same way. And then the chapters, then the books, and so on until the unity of the Bible is found on its own terms.

I felt like my little brown path of life had entered an orchard, a vineyard, a garden with mind-blowing, heart-thrilling, life-changing fruit to be picked everywhere. Never had I seen so much truth and so much beauty condensed in so small a sphere. The Bible seemed to me then, and it seems today, inexhaustible. This is what I had dreamed about in the health center with mono, when God called me to the ministry of the Word. Now the question became: What is the Point, the Purpose, the Focus, the Essence of this beautiful glimpse of divine Truth?

A GLIMPSE OF WHY I AND EVERYTHING EXIST

In course after course the pieces were put in place. What a gift those three years of seminary were! In the final class with Dr. Fuller, called "The Unity of the Bible" (which is also a book by that title[3]) the unifying flag was hoisted over the whole Bible.

> God ordained a redemptive history whose sequence fully displays his glory so that, at the end, the greatest possible number of people would have had the historical antecedents necessary to engender [the most] fervent love for God. . . . The one thing God is doing in all of redemptive history is to

show forth his mercy in such a way that the greatest number of people will throughout eternity delight in him with all their heart, strength, and mind. . . . When the earth of the new creation is filled with such people, then God's purpose in showing forth his mercy will have been achieved. . . . All the events of redemptive history and their meaning as recorded in the Bible compose a unity in that they conjoin to bring about this goal.[4]

Contained in these sentences were the seeds of my future. The driving passion of my life was rooted here. One of the seeds was in the word "glory"—God's aim in history was to "fully display his glory." Another seed was in the word "delight"—God's aim was that his people "delight in him with all their heart." The passion of my life has been to understand and live and teach and preach how these two aims of God relate to each other—indeed, how they are not two but one.

It was becoming clearer and clearer that if I wanted to come to the end of my life and not say, "I've wasted it!" then I would need to press all the way in, and all the way up, to the ultimate purpose of God and join him in it. If my life was to have a single, all-satisfying, unifying passion, it would have to be God's passion. And, if Daniel Fuller was right, God's passion was the display of his own glory and the delight of my heart.

All of my life since that discovery has been spent experiencing and examining and explaining that truth. It has become clearer and more certain and more demanding with every year. It has become clearer that God being glorified and God being enjoyed are not separate categories. They relate to each other not like fruit and animals, but like fruit and apples. Apples are one kind of fruit. Enjoying God supremely is one way to glorify him. Enjoying God makes him look supremely valuable.

AN EIGHTEENTH-CENTURY PREACHER SEALED THE BREAKTHROUGH

Jonathan Edwards came into my life at this time with the most powerful confirmation of this truth I have ever seen outside the Bible. It was powerful because he showed that it was in the Bible. In 2003 we marked his 300th birthday. He was a pastor and theologian in New England. For me he has become the most important dead teacher outside the Bible. No one outside Scripture has shaped my vision of God and the Christian life more than Jonathan Edwards.

I thank God that Edwards did not waste his life. It ended abruptly from a failed smallpox vaccination when he was fifty-four. But he had lived well. His life is inspiring because of his zeal not to waste it, and because of his passion for the supremacy of God. Consider some of the resolutions he wrote in his early twenties to intensify his life for the glory of God.

- Resolution #5: "Resolved, never to lose one moment of time; but improve it the most profitable way I possibly can."
- Resolution #6: "Resolved, to live with all my might, while I do live."
- Resolution #17: "Resolved, that I will live so, as I shall wish I had done when I come to die."
- Resolution #22: "Resolved, to endeavor to obtain for myself as much happiness, in the other world, as I possibly can, with all the power, might, vigor, and vehemence, yea violence, I am capable of, or can bring myself to exert, in any way that can be thought of."[5]

This last resolution (#22) may strike us as blatantly self-centered, even dangerous, if we do not understand the deep connection in Edwards's mind between the glory of God and the happiness of Christians. The violence he had in mind was what Jesus meant when he said in essence, "Better to gouge out your eye to kill lust and go to heaven than to make peace with sin and go to hell" (Matthew 5:29). And with regard to seeking his own happiness, keep in mind that Edwards was absolutely convinced that being happy in God was the way we glorify him. This was the reason we were created. Delighting in God was not a mere preference or option in life; it was our joyful duty and should be the single passion of our lives. Therefore to resolve to maximize his happiness in God was to resolve to show him more glorious than all other sources of happiness. Seeking happiness in God and glorifying God were the same.

THE GREAT COMING TOGETHER FOR ME

Here is how Edwards explained it. He preached a sermon when he was still in his early twenties with this main point: "The godly are designed for unknown and inconceivable happiness." His text was 1 John 3:2, "And it doth not yet appear what we shall be" (KJV).

> [The] glory of God [does not] consist merely in the creature's perceiving his perfections: for the creature may perceive the power and wisdom of God, and yet take no delight in it, but abhor it. Those creatures that so do, don't glorify God. Nor doth the glory of God consist especially in speaking of his perfections: for words avail not any otherwise than as they express the sentiment of the mind. This glory of God, therefore, [consists] in the creature's admiring and rejoicing [and] exulting in the manifestation of his beauty and excellency. . . . The essence of glorifying . . . God consists, therefore, in the creature's rejoicing in God's manifestations of his beauty, which is the joy and happiness we speak of. So we see it comes to this at last: that the end of the creation is that God may communicate happiness to the creature; for if God created the world that he may be glorified in the creature,

he created it that they might rejoice in his glory: for we have shown that they are the same.[6]

This was the great coming together for me—the break-through. What was life about? What was it for? Why do I exist? Why am I here? To be happy? Or to glorify God? Unspoken for years, there was in me the feeling that these two were at odds. Either you glorify God or you pursue happiness. One seemed absolutely right; the other seemed absolutely inevitable. And that is why I was confused and frustrated for so long.

Compounding the problem was that many who seemed to emphasize the glory of God in their thinking did not seem to enjoy him much. And many who seemed to enjoy God most were defective in their thinking about his glory. But now here was the greatest mind of early America, Jonathan Edwards, say-ing that God's purpose for my life was that I have a passion for God's glory and that I have a passion for my joy in that glory, and that these two are one passion.

When I saw this, I knew, at last, what a wasted life would be and how to avoid it.

God created me—and you—to live with a single, all-embrac-ing, all-transforming passion—namely, a passion to glorify God by enjoying and displaying his supreme excellence in all the spheres of life. Enjoying and displaying are both crucial. If we try to display the excellence of God without joy in it, we will display a shell of hypocrisy and create scorn or legalism. But if we claim to enjoy his excellence and do not display it for oth-ers to see and admire, we deceive ourselves, because the mark of God-enthralled joy is to overflow and expand by extending itself into the hearts of others. The wasted life is the life without a passion for the supremacy of God in all things for the joy of all peoples.

THE CRYSTAL-CLEAR REASON FOR LIVING

The Bible is crystal-clear: God created us for his glory. Thus says the Lord, "Bring my sons from afar and my daughters from the end of the earth, everyone who is called by my name, whom *I created for my glory*" (Isaiah 43:6-7). Life is wasted when we do not live for the glory of God. And I mean *all* of life. It is all for his glory. That is why the Bible gets down into the details of eating and drinking. "Whether you eat or drink, or whatever you do, *do all to the glory of God*" (1 Corinthians 10:31). We waste our lives when we do not weave God into our eating and drinking and every other part by enjoying and displaying him.

What does it mean to glorify God? It may get a dangerous twist if we are not careful. *Glorify* is like the word *beautify*. But *beautify* usually means "make something more beautiful than it is," improve its beauty. That is emphatically *not* what we mean by *glorify* in relation to God. God cannot be made more glorious or more beautiful than he is. He cannot be improved, "nor is he served by human hands, as though he needed anything" (Acts 17:25). *Glorify* does not mean add more glory to God.

It is more like the word *magnify*. But here too we can go wrong. *Magnify* has two distinct meanings. In relation to God, one is worship and one is wickedness. You can magnify like a telescope or like a microscope. When you magnify like a microscope, you make something tiny look bigger than it is. A dust mite can look like a monster. Pretending to magnify God like that is wickedness. But when you magnify like a telescope, you make something unimaginably great look like what it really is. With the Hubble Space Telescope, pinprick galaxies in the sky are revealed for the billion-star giants that they are. Magnifying God like that is worship.

We waste our lives when we do not pray and think and dream and plan and work toward magnifying God in all spheres of life. God created us for this: to live our lives in a way that makes him look more like the greatness and the beauty and the infinite worth that he really is. In the night sky of this world God appears to most people, if at all, like a pinprick of light in a heaven of darkness. But he created us and called us to make him look like what he really is. This is what it means to be created in the image of God. We are meant to image forth in the world what he is really like.

DOES BEING LOVED MEAN BEING MADE MUCH OF?

For many people, this is not obviously an act of love. They do not feel loved when they are told that God created them for *his* glory. They feel used. This is understandable given the way love has been almost completely distorted in our world. For most people, to be loved is to be made much of. Almost everything in our Western culture serves this distortion of love. We are taught in a thousand ways that love means increasing someone's self-esteem. Love is helping someone feel good about themselves. Love is giving someone a mirror and helping him like what he sees.

This is not what the Bible means by the love of God. Love is doing what is best for someone. But making self the object of our highest affections is not best for us. It is, in fact, a lethal distraction. We were made to see and savor God—and savoring him, to be supremely satisfied, and thus spread in all the world the worth of his presence. Not to show people the all-satisfying God is not to love them. To make them feel good about themselves when they were made to feel good about seeing God is like taking someone to the Alps and locking them in a room full of mirrors.

PATHOLOGICAL AT THE GRAND CANYON

The really wonderful moments of joy in this world are not the moments of self-satisfaction, but self-forgetfulness. Standing on the edge of the Grand Canyon and contemplating your own greatness is pathological. At such moments we are made for a magnificent joy that comes from outside ourselves. And each of these rare and precious moments in life—beside the Canyon, before the Alps, under the stars—is an echo of a far greater excellence, namely, the glory of God. That is why the Bible says, "The heavens declare the glory of God, and the sky above proclaims his handiwork" (Psalm 19:1).

Sometimes people say that they cannot believe that, if there is a God, he would take interest in such a tiny speck of reality called humanity on Planet Earth. The universe, they say, is so vast, it makes man utterly insignificant. Why would God have bothered to create such a microscopic speck called the earth and humanity and then get involved with us?

Beneath this question is a fundamental failure to see what the universe is about. It is about the greatness of God, not the significance of man. God made man small and the universe big to say something about himself. And he says it for us to learn and enjoy—namely, that he is infinitely great and powerful and wise and beautiful. The more the Hubble Telescope sends back to us about the unfathomable depths of space, the more we should stand in awe of God. The disproportion between us and the universe is a parable about the disproportion between us and God. And it is an understatement. But the point is not to nullify us but to glorify him.

LOVING PEOPLE MEANS POINTING THEM TO THE ALL-SATISFYING GOD

Now back to what it means to be loved. The idea has been almost totally distorted. Love has to do with showing a dying soul the life-giving beauty of the glory of God, especially his grace. Yes, as we will see, we show God's glory in a hundred practical ways that include care about food and clothes and shelter and health. That's what Jesus meant when he said, "Let your light shine before others, so that they may see your *good works* and give glory to your Father who is in heaven" (Matthew 5:16).

Every good work should be a revelation of the glory of God. What makes the good deed an act of love is not the raw act, but the passion and the sacrifice to make God himself known as glorious. Not to aim to show God is not to love, because God is what we need most deeply. And to have all else without him is to perish in the end. The Bible says that you can give away all that you have and deliver your body to be burned and have not love (1 Corinthians 13:3). If you don't point people to God for everlasting joy, you don't love. You waste your life.

IS ETERNAL LIFE A HEAVEN FULL OF MIRRORS?

Now think what this means for God's love. How shall God love us? Mere logic could give us the answer: God loves us best by giving us the best to enjoy forever, namely himself, for he is best. But we are not dependent on logic alone. The Bible makes this clear. "For God so loved the world, that he gave his only Son, that whoever believes in him should not perish but have eternal life" (John 3:16). God loves us by giving us *eternal life* at the cost of his Son, Jesus Christ. But what is eternal life? Is it eternal self-esteem? Is it a heaven full of mirrors? Or snowboards, or golf links, or black-eyed virgins?

No. Jesus tells us exactly what he meant: "And this is eternal life, that they know you the only true God, and Jesus Christ whom you have sent" (John 17:3). What is eternal life? It is to know God and his Son, Jesus Christ. No thing can satisfy the soul. The soul was made to stand in awe of a Person—the only person worthy of awe. All heroes are shadows of Christ. We love to admire their excellence. How much more will we be satisfied by the one Person who conceived all excellence and embodies all skill, all talent, all strength and brilliance and savvy and goodness. This is what I have been trying to say. God loves us by liberating us from the bondage of self so that we can enjoy knowing and admiring him forever.

Or consider the way the apostle Peter says it. "Christ also suffered once for sins, the righteous for the unrighteous, *that he might bring us to God*" (1 Peter 3:18). Why did God send Jesus Christ to die for us? "That he might bring us to God"—to himself. God sent Christ to die so that we could come home to the all-satisfying Father. This is love. God's love for us is God's doing what he must do, at great cost to himself, so that we might have the pleasure of seeing and savoring him forever. If it is true, as the Psalmist says to God, "In your presence there is fullness of joy; at your right hand are pleasures forevermore" (Psalm 16:11), then what must love do? It must rescue us from our addiction to self and bring us, changed, into the presence of God.

ARE YOU BEING USED?

So here is the question to test whether you have been sucked into this world's distortion of love: Would you feel more loved by God if he made much of you, or if he liberated you from the bondage of self-regard, at great cost to himself, so that you enjoy making much of him forever?

Suppose you answer, "I want to be free from self and full of joy in God; I want to enjoy making much of God, not me. And I want the fullness of my joy to last forever." If you respond this way, then you will also have an answer to the fear I mentioned earlier, that you are just being used by God when he creates you for his glory. Now we see that in creating us for his glory, he is creating us for our highest joy. He is most glorified in us when we are most satisfied in him.

God is the one being in the universe for whom self-exaltation is the most loving act. Anyone else who exalts himself distracts us from what we need, namely, God. But if God exalts himself, he calls attention to the very thing we need most for our joy. If great paintings could talk, and they saw you walking through the gallery staring at the floor, they would cry out, "Look! Look at me. I am the reason you are here." And when you look and exult in the beauty of the paintings with those around you, your joy would be full. You would not complain that the paintings should have kept quiet. They rescued you from wasting your visit. In the same way no child complains, "I am being used" when his father delights to make the child happy with his own presence.

FINALLY FREE TO EMBRACE THE SINGLE PASSION FOR WHICH I WAS MADE

With these discoveries I now felt free to affirm God's purpose for my life revealed in the Bible. I didn't have to be afraid that I must choose between what is right and what is inevitable—between pursuing his glory and pursuing my joy. I was free to experience the single passion for God's supremacy in all things for the joy of all peoples. I was rescued from the wasted life. Now life could have ultimate meaning—the same meaning God's life has: enjoying and displaying his greatness.

I was free to embrace the end of my old quest: the Point, the Purpose, the Focus, and the Essence of it all. It was real. It was objective. It was there. And it was rooted in the very essence of what God is in himself. He is glorious, beautiful, and magnificent in his manifold perfections. They are infinite, eternal, and unchanging. They are Truth and Justice and Goodness and Wisdom and Power and Love. Flowing out from what he is in himself comes the purpose for our existence. God's passion for his own glory gives birth to ours. That is the single, all-embracing, all-transforming reason for being: a passion to enjoy and display God's supremacy in all things for the joy of all peoples.

God created us to live with a single passion to joyfully display his supreme excellence in all the spheres of life. The wasted life is the life without this passion. God calls us to pray and think and dream and plan and work not to be made much of, but to make much of him in every part of our lives.

NOW ENTERS THE GLORY OF JESUS CHRIST

Since September 11, 2001, I have seen more clearly than ever how essential it is to exult explicitly in the excellence of Christ crucified for sinners and risen from the dead. Christ must be explicit in all our God-talk. It will not do, in this day of pluralism, to talk about the glory of God in vague ways. God without Christ is no God. And a no-God cannot save or satisfy the soul. Following a no-God—whatever his name or whatever his religion—will be a wasted life. God-in-Christ is the only true God and the only path to joy. Everything I have said so far must now be related to Christ. The old kitchen plaque comes back: "Only what's done for Christ will last."

To bring us to this highest and most durable of all pleasures, God made his Son, Jesus Christ, a bloody spectacle of blameless suffering and death. This is what it cost to rescue us from a wasted life. The eternal Son of God "did not count equality with God a thing to be grasped, but made himself nothing." He took "the form of a servant" and was born "in the likeness of men. . . . He humbled himself by becoming obedient to the point of death, even death on a cross" (Philippians 2:6-8).

ALL THINGS WERE MADE FOR HIM

This Jesus was and is a real historical man in whom "the whole fullness of deity dwells bodily" (Colossians 2:9). Since he is

"God of God, Light of Light, very God of very God," as the old Nicene Creed says, and since his death and resurrection are the central act of God in history, it is not surprising to hear the Bible say, "All things were created through him and *for him*" (Colossians 1:16). For *him*! That means for his glory. Which also means that everything we have said so far about God creating us for his glory also means that he created us for the glory of his Son.

In his prayer in John 17 the first thing Jesus asks is, "Father, the hour has come; glorify your Son that the Son may glorify you" (John 17:1). Ever since the incarnate, redeeming work of Jesus, God is gladly glorified by sinners only through the glorification of the risen God-Man, Jesus Christ. His bloody death is the blazing center of the glory of God. There is no way to the glory of the Father but through the Son. All the promises of joy in God's presence, and pleasures at his right hand, come to us only through faith in Jesus Christ.

IF WE REJECT HIM, WE REJECT GOD

Jesus is the litmus test of reality for all persons and all religions. He said it clearly: "The one who rejects me rejects him who sent me" (Luke 10:16). People and religions who reject Christ reject God. Do other religions know the true God? Here is the test: Do they reject Jesus as the only Savior for sinners who was crucified and raised by God from the dead? If they do, they do not know God in a saving way.

That is what Jesus meant when he said, "I am the way, and the truth, and the life. No one comes to the Father except through me" (John 14:6). Or when he said, "Whoever does not honor the Son does not honor the Father who sent him" (John 5:23). Or when he said to the Pharisees, "If God were your Father, you would love me" (John 8:42).

It's what the apostle John meant when he said, "No one

who denies the Son has the Father. Whoever confesses the Son has the Father also" (1 John 2:23). Or when he said, "Everyone who . . . does not abide in the teaching of Christ, does not have God" (2 John 9).

There is no point in romanticizing other religions that reject the deity and saving work of Christ. They do not know God. And those who follow them tragically waste their lives.

If we would see and savor the glory of God, we must see and savor Christ. For Christ is "the image of the invisible God" (Colossians 1:15). To put it another way, if we would embrace the glory of God, we must embrace the Gospel of Christ. The reason for this is not only because we are sinners and need a Savior to die for us, but also because this Savior is himself the fullest and most beautiful manifestation of the glory of God. He purchases our undeserved and everlasting pleasure, and he becomes for us our all-deserving, everlasting Treasure.

THE GOSPEL IS THE GOOD NEWS OF THE GLORY OF CHRIST

This is how the Gospel is defined. When we are converted through faith in Christ, what we see with the eyes of our hearts is "the light of the gospel of the glory of Christ, who is the image of God" (2 Corinthians 4:4). The Gospel is the good news of all-conquering beauty. Or to say it the way Paul does, it is the good news of "the glory of Christ." When we embrace Christ, we embrace God. We see and savor God's glory. There is no savoring of God's glory if we do not see it in Christ. This is the only window through which a sinner may see the face of God and not be incinerated.

The Bible says that when God illuminates our heart at conversion, he gives "the light of the knowledge of the glory of God in the face of Jesus Christ" (2 Corinthians 4:6). Either we see the glory of God "in the face of Jesus Christ," or we don't see it at all. And the "face of Jesus Christ" is the beauty of Christ reaching its climax in the cross. The bloody face of Christ crucified (and triumphant!) is the countenance of the glory of God. What was once foolishness to us becomes our wisdom and our power and our boast (1 Corinthians 1:18, 24).

Life is wasted if we do not grasp the glory of the cross, cherish it for the treasure that it is, and cleave to it as the highest price of every pleasure and the deepest comfort in every pain. That is what the next chapter is about.

NOTES

1 E. D. Hirsch, *Validity in Interpretation* (New Haven, Conn.: Yale University Press, 1967), ix. This quote does not reflect what Hirsch believes but what he is arguing against.

2 The quote is from aphorism 125 titled "The Madman," in *The Joyful Science*, cited in Damon Linker, "Nietzsche's Truth," *First Things* 125 (August/September, 2002): 54; available online at http://www.firstthings.com/ftissues/ft0208/articles/linker.html.

3 Daniel Fuller, *The Unity of the Bible: Unfolding God's Plan for Humanity* (Grand Rapids, Mich.: Zondervan, 1992).

4 Ibid., 453-454.

5 Jonathan Edwards, *The Works of Jonathan Edwards*, Vol. 1 (Edinburgh: Banner of Truth, 1976), xx-xxi.

6 Jonathan Edwards, "Nothing Upon Earth Can Represent the Glories of Heaven," in *The Works of Jonathan Edwards*, Vol. 14, ed. Kenneth P. Minkema (New Haven, Conn.: Yale University Press, 1997), 144.

CHAPTER 3

BOASTING ONLY IN THE CROSS, THE BLAZING CENTER OF THE GLORY OF GOD

$\mathcal{J}$he opposite of wasting your life is living life by a single God-exalting, soul-satisfying passion. The well-lived life must be God-exalting and soul-satisfying because that is why God created us (Isaiah 43:7; Psalm 90:14). That was the burden of Chapter 2. And "passion" is the right word (or, if you prefer, zeal, fervor, ardor, blood-earnestness) because God commands us to love him with *all* our heart (Matthew 22:37), and Jesus reminds us that he spits lukewarm people out of his mouth (Revelation 3:16). The opposite of wasting your life is to live by a single, soul-satisfying passion for the supremacy of God in all things.

How serious is this word "single"? Can life really have that much "singleness" of purpose? Can work and leisure and relationships and eating and lovemaking and ministry all really flow from a single passion? Is there something deep enough and big enough and strong enough to hold all that together? Can sex and cars and work and war and changing diapers and doing taxes really have a God-exalting, soul-satisfying unity?

This question drives us to the very same place where we ended Chapter 2, namely, to the death of Jesus on the cross. We ended there because living for the glory of God must mean living for the glory of Christ crucified. Christ is the image of God. He is the sum of God's glory in human form. And his beauty shines most brightly at his darkest hour.

PRESSED BY THE BIBLE TO KNOW ONE THING

But we are driven to the same bloody place also by the question of a *single* passion. The Bible pushes us in this direction. For example, the apostle Paul said that his life and ministry were riveted on a single aim: "I decided to know nothing among you except Jesus Christ and him crucified" (1 Corinthians 2:2). That is astonishing, when you think of all the varied things Paul did, in fact, talk about. There must be a sense in which "Jesus Christ and him crucified" is the ground and sum of everything else he says. He is pushing us to see our lives with a single focus, and for the cross of Christ to be that focus.

You don't have to know a lot of things for your life to make a lasting difference in the world. But you do have to know the few great things that matter, perhaps just one, and then be willing to live for them and die for them. The people that make a durable difference in the world are not the people who have mastered many things, but who have been mastered by one great thing. If you want your life to count, if you want the ripple effect of the pebbles you drop to become waves that reach the ends of the earth and roll on into eternity, you don't need to have a high IQ. You don't have to have good looks or riches or come from a fine family or a fine school. Instead you have to know a few great, majestic, unchanging, obvious, simple, glorious things—or one great all-embracing thing—and be set on fire by them.

A TRAGEDY IN THE MAKING

You may not be sure that you want your life to make a difference. Maybe you don't care very much whether you make a lasting difference for the sake of something great. You just want people to like you. If people would just like being around you, you'd be satisfied. Or if you could just have a good job with a good wife, or husband, and a couple of good kids and a nice car and long weekends and a few good friends, a fun retirement, and a quick and easy death, and no hell—if you could have all that (even without God)—you would be satisfied. That is a tragedy in the making. A wasted life.

THESE LIVES AND DEATHS WERE NO TRAGEDY

In April 2000, Ruby Eliason and Laura Edwards were killed in Cameroon, West Africa. Ruby was over eighty. Single all her life, she poured it out for one great thing: to make Jesus Christ known among the unreached, the poor, and the sick. Laura was a widow, a medical doctor, pushing eighty years old, and serving at Ruby's side in Cameroon. The brakes failed, the car went over a cliff, and they were both killed instantly. I asked my congregation: Was that a tragedy? Two lives, driven by one great passion, namely, to be spent in unheralded service to the perishing poor for the glory of Jesus Christ—even two decades after most of their American counterparts had retired to throw away their lives on trifles. No, that is not a tragedy. That is a glory. These lives were not wasted. And these lives were not lost. "Whoever loses his life for my sake and the gospel's will save it" (Mark 8:35).

AN AMERICAN TRAGEDY: HOW NOT TO FINISH YOUR ONE LIFE

I will tell you what a tragedy is. I will show you how to waste your life. Consider a story from the February 1998 edition of *Reader's Digest*, which tells about a couple who "took early retirement from their jobs in the Northeast five years ago when he was 59 and she was 51. Now they live in Punta Gorda, Florida, where they cruise on their 30 foot trawler, play softball and collect shells." At first, when I read it I thought it might be a joke. A spoof on the American Dream. But it wasn't. Tragically, this was the dream: Come to the end of your life—your one and only precious, God-given life—and let the last great work of your life, before you give an account to your Creator, be this: playing softball and collecting shells. Picture them before Christ at the great day of judgment: "Look, Lord. See my shells." *That* is a tragedy. And people today are spending billions of dollars to persuade you to embrace that tragic dream. Over against that, I put my protest: Don't buy it. Don't waste your life.

PRETEND I AM YOUR FATHER

As I write this, I am now in my sixties. As the months go by, I relate to more and more people who are young enough to be my sons and daughters. You may be in that category. I have four sons and one daughter. Few things, if any, fill me with more longing these months and years than the longing that my children not waste their lives on fatal success.

This longing transfers very easily to you, especially if you are in your twenties or thirties. I see you, as it were, like a son or a daughter, and in these pages I plead with you as a father—perhaps a father who loves you dearly, or the father you never had. Or the father who never had a vision for you like I have for you—and God has for you. Or the father who *has* a vision for you, but it's all about money and status. I look through these pages and see you as sons and daughters, and I plead with you: Desire that your life count for something great! Long for your life to have eternal significance. Want this! Don't coast through life without a passion.

I LOVE THE VISION OF LOUIE GIGLIO

One of the inspirations behind this book was my participation in the conferences for college students and young adults called Passion '97, Passion '98, Passion '99, OneDay (2002), and OneDay03. Under Christ, the spark plug behind these worship and mission-mobilizing gatherings was Louie Giglio. He is calling young people to make a "268 Declaration." The number comes from Isaiah 26:8—"Yes, LORD, walking in the way of your laws, we wait for you; your name and renown are the desire of our hearts" (NIV). The first statement of the "Declaration" says, "Because I was created by God and for His glory, I will magnify Him as I respond to His great love. My desire is to make knowing and enjoying God the passionate pursuit of my life."[1]

This vision of life holds out to students and young adults so much more than the emptiness of mere success or the orgy of spring break. Here is not just a body, but a soul. Not just a soul, but a soul with a passion and a desire. Not just a desire for being liked or for playing softball or collecting shells. Here is a desire for something infinitely great and beautiful and valuable and satisfying—the name and the glory of God—"Your name and renown are the desire of our hearts."

This accords with everything I wrote in the last chapter and applies it to the upcoming generation. This is what I live to know and long to experience. This is virtually the mission statement of my life and the church I serve: "We exist to spread a passion for the supremacy of God in all things for the joy of all peoples through Jesus Christ." You don't have to say it like I say it or like Louie Giglio says it. But whatever you do, find the God-centered, Christ-exalting, Bible-saturated passion of your life, and find your way to say it and live for it and die for it. And you will make a difference that lasts. You will not waste your life.

THE MAN WHOSE SINGLE PASSION MADE ALL ELSE RUBBISH

You will be like the apostle Paul, as we saw earlier, when he said that he wanted to know nothing but Jesus Christ and him crucified. Nobody had a more single-minded vision for his life than Paul did. He could say it in many different ways. He could say: "I do not account my life of any value nor as precious to myself, if only I may finish my course and the ministry that I received from the Lord Jesus, to testify to the gospel of the grace of God" (Acts 20:24). One thing mattered: "I will not waste my life! I will finish my course and finish it well. I will display the Gospel of the grace of God in all I do. I will run my race to the end."

Or he could say, "Whatever gain I had, I counted as loss for the sake of Christ. Indeed, I count everything as loss because of the surpassing worth of knowing Christ Jesus my Lord. For his sake I have suffered the loss of all things and count them as rubbish, in order that I may gain Christ" (Philippians 3:7-8). One thing matters: Know Christ, and gain Christ. Everything is rubbish in comparison to this.

What is the one passion of your life that makes everything else look like rubbish in comparison? Oh, that God would help me waken in you a single passion for a single great reality that would unleash you, and set you free from small dreams, and send you, for the glory of Christ, into all the spheres of secular life and to all the peoples of the earth.

CHRIST CRUCIFIED, THE BLAZING CENTER OF THE GLORY OF GOD

With a prayer to that end, I take up again where I left off in the last chapter. There I said, "Life is wasted if we do not grasp the glory of the cross, cherish it for the treasure that it is, and cleave to it as the highest price of every pleasure and the deepest comfort in every pain." What was once foolishness to us—a crucified God—must become our wisdom and our power and our only boast in this world.

I argued in Chapter 2 that God created us to live for his glory, and that God is most glorified in us when we are most satisfied in him. We magnify God's worth the most when *he* becomes our only boast. And I concluded that chapter with a claim that his glory can only be seen and savored by sinners through the glory of Jesus Christ. Any other approach to God is illusion or incineration. If we would make much of God, we must make much of Christ. His bloody death is the blazing center of the glory of God. If God is to be our boast, what he did and what he is in Christ must be our boast.

THE SHOCKING SUMMONS TO BOAST IN A LYNCHING ROPE

In this regard, few verses in the Bible are more radical and sweeping and Christ-exalting than Galatians 6:14: "Far be it from me to boast except in the cross of our Lord Jesus Christ, by which the world has been crucified to me, and I to the world." Or to state it positively: Only boast in the cross of Jesus Christ. This is a single idea. A single goal for life. A single passion. Only boast in the cross. The word "boast" can be translated "exult in" or "rejoice in." Only exult in the cross of Christ. Only rejoice in the cross of Christ. Paul says, Let this be your single passion, your single boast and joy and exultation. If you understand me—and

49

I hope you will before we are done—you will know why it does not contradict but confirms all I have written in Chapter 2 when I pray for you, the reader, *May the one thing that you cherish, the one thing that you rejoice in and exult over, be the cross of Jesus Christ.*

For Paul to say that we should boast only in the cross of Christ is shocking for two reasons.

One is that it's like saying: Boast only in the electric chair. Only exult in the gas chamber. Only rejoice in the lethal injection. Let your one boast and one joy and one exultation be the lynching rope. "May it never be that I would boast, except in the cross of our Lord Jesus Christ." No manner of execution that has ever been devised was more cruel and agonizing than to be nailed to a cross and hung up to die like a piece of meat. It was horrible. You would not have been able to watch it—not without screaming and pulling at your hair and tearing your clothes. You probably would have vomited. Let this, Paul says, be the one passion of your life. That is one thing that is shocking about his words.

The other is that he says this is to be the *only* boast of your life. The only joy. The only exultation. "Far be it from me to boast except in the cross of our Lord Jesus Christ, by which the world has been crucified to me, and I to the world." What does he mean by this? Can he be serious? No other boast? No other exultation? No other joy except the cross of Jesus?

What about the places where Paul himself uses the same word to talk about boasting or exulting in other things? For example, Romans 5:2: "We *rejoice* in hope of the glory of God." Romans 5:3-4: "More than that, we *rejoice* in our sufferings, knowing that suffering produces endurance, and endurance produces character, and character produces hope." Second Corinthians 12:9: "I will *boast* all the more gladly of my weaknesses, so that the power of Christ may rest upon me." First Thessalonians

2:19: "What is our hope or joy or crown of *boasting* before our Lord Jesus at his coming? Is it not you?"

"BOAST ONLY IN THIS" MEANS "LET ALL BOASTING BE BOASTING IN THIS"

So, if Paul can boast and exult and rejoice in all these things, what does Paul mean—that he would not "boast except in the cross of our Lord Jesus Christ"? Is that just double-talk? You exult in one thing, but say that you are exulting in another thing? No. There is a very profound reason for saying that all exultation, all rejoicing, all boasting in anything should be a rejoicing in the cross of Jesus Christ.

Paul means something that will change every part of your life. He means that, for the Christian, all other boasting should also be a boasting in the cross. All exultation in anything else should be exultation in the cross. If you exult in the hope of glory, you should be exulting in the cross of Christ. If you exult in tribulation because tribulation works hope, you should be exulting in the cross of Christ. If you exult in your weaknesses, or in the people of God, you should be exulting in the cross of Christ.

CHRIST BOUGHT EVERY GOOD THING AND EVERY BAD THING THAT TURNED FOR GOOD

Why is this the case? Because for redeemed sinners, every good thing—indeed every bad thing that God turns for good—was obtained for us by the cross of Christ. Apart from the death of Christ, sinners get nothing but judgment. Apart from the cross of Christ, there is only condemnation. Therefore everything that you enjoy in Christ—as a Christian, as a person who trusts Christ—is owing to the death of Christ. And all your rejoicing in all things should therefore be a rejoicing in the cross where all your blessings were purchased for you at the cost of the death of the Son of God, Jesus Christ.

One of the reasons we are not as Christ-centered and cross-saturated as we should be is that we have not realized that everything—everything good, and everything bad that God turns for the good of his redeemed children—was purchased by the death of Christ for us. We simply take life and breath and health and friends and everything for granted. We think it is ours by right. But the fact is that it is not ours by right. We are doubly undeserving of it.

1) We are *creatures*, and our Creator is not bound or obligated to give us anything—not life or health or anything. He gives, he takes, and he does us no injustice (Job 1:21).

2) And besides being creatures with no claim on our Creator, we are *sinners*. We have fallen short of his glory (Romans 3:23). We have ignored him and disobeyed him and failed to love him and trust him. The wrath of his justice is kindled against us. All we deserve from him is judgment (Romans 3:19). Therefore every breath we take, every time our heart beats, every day that the sun rises, every moment we see with our eyes or hear with our ears or speak with our mouths or walk with our legs is, for now, a free and undeserved gift to sinners who deserve only judgment.

WELCOMED MERCY OR MOUNTING WRATH?

I say "for now" because if you refuse to see God in his gifts, they will turn out not to be gifts but High Court evidence of ingratitude. The Bible speaks of them first as "the riches of his kindness and forbearance and patience" that point us to repentance (Romans 2:4). But when we presume upon them and do not cherish God's grace in them, "Because of your hard and impenitent heart you are storing up wrath for yourself on the day of wrath when God's righteous judgment will be revealed" (Romans 2:5).

But for those who see the merciful hand of God in every breath they take and give credit where it is due, Jesus Christ will be seen and savored as the great Purchaser of every undeserved breath. Every heartbeat will be received as a gift from his hand.

DESERVING NOTHING BUT INHERITING EVERYTHING—WHY?

How then did he purchase them? Answer: by his blood. If I deserve nothing but condemnation because of my sin, but instead get life and breath in this age, and everlasting joy in the age to come, because Christ died for me, then everything good—and everything bad that God turns for good—must be the reward of his suffering (not my merit). This includes all that diversity that I wondered about at the beginning of this chapter. I asked, can work and leisure and relationships and eating and lovemaking and ministry all really flow from a single passion? Is there something deep enough and big enough and strong enough to hold all that together? Can sex and cars and work and war and changing diapers and doing taxes really have a God-exalting, soul-satisfying unity? Now we see that every experience in life is designed to magnify the cross of Christ. Or to say it another way, every good thing in life (or bad thing graciously turned for good) is meant to magnify Christ and him crucified.

DID CHRIST BUY MY TOTALED DODGE?

So, for example, we totaled our old Dodge Spirit several years ago, but nobody was hurt. And in that safety I exult. I glory in that. But why was nobody hurt? That was a gift to me and my family that none of us deserves. And it won't always be that way. But this time it was, and we didn't deserve it. We are sinners and by nature children of wrath, apart from Christ. So how did we come to have such a gift for our good? Answer: Christ died for our sins on the cross and took away the wrath of God from us and secured for us, even though we don't deserve it, God's omnipotent grace that works everything together for our good. So when I exult in our safety, I am exulting in the cross of Christ.

Then the insurance paid us for the car, and my wife Noël took that money and went to Iowa and bought a Chevy Lumina that was one year newer and drove it home in the snow. And I exult in the amazing grace of so much bounty. Just like that. You wreck your car. You come out unhurt. Insurance pays up. You get another one. And you move on almost as if nothing had happened. And in thanks I bow my head and exult in the untold mercies even of these little material things. Where do all these mercies come from? If you are a saved sinner, a believer in Jesus, they come through the cross. Apart from the cross, there is only judgment—patience and mercy for a season, but then, if spurned, all that mercy only serves to intensify judgment. Therefore every good thing in life, and every bad thing that God turns for good, is a blood-bought gift. And all boasting—all exultation—should be boasting in the cross.

Woe to me if I exult in any blessing of any kind at any time, unless my exulting is an exulting in the cross of Christ.

Another way to say this is that the design of the cross is the glory of Christ. The aim of God in the cross is that Christ would be honored. When Paul says in Galatians 6:14, "Far be it from me to boast except in the cross of our Lord Jesus Christ," he is saying that God's will is that the cross always be magnified— that Christ crucified always be our boast and exultation and joy and praise—that Christ get glory and thanks and honor for every good thing in our lives and every bad thing that God turns for good.

SPREADING A PASSION FOR CHRIST CRUCIFIED— BY TEACHING

But now here's a question: If that is the aim of God in the death of Christ—namely, that "Christ crucified" be honored and glorified for all things—then *how* is Christ to get the glory he deserves? The answer is that this generation has to be taught that these things are so. Or to say it another way: The source of exultation in the cross of Christ is education about the cross of Christ.

That's my job. I am not alone, but I do embrace it for myself with a passion. This is what I believe the Lord called me to in 1966 when I lay sick with mono in the health center in Wheaton, Illinois. This is where it was all leading—God's mandate: So live and so study and so serve and so preach and so write that Jesus Christ, the crucified and risen God, be the only boast of this generation. And if this is my job, yours is the same, just in a different form: to live and speak in such a way that the worth of "Christ crucified" is seen and savored by more and more people. It will be costly for us as it was for him.

THE ONLY PLACE TO BOAST IN THE CROSS IS ON THE CROSS

If we desire that there be no boasting except in the cross, then we must live near the cross—indeed we must live on the cross. This is shocking. But this is what Galatians 6:14 says: "Far be it from me to boast except in the cross of our Lord Jesus Christ, *by which the world has been crucified to me, and I to the world.*" Boasting *in* the cross happens when you are *on* the cross. Is that not what Paul says? "The world has been crucified to me, and I [have been crucified] to the world." The world is dead to me, and I am dead to the world. Why? Because I have been crucified. We learn to boast in the cross and exult in the cross when we are on the cross. And until our selves are crucified there, our boast will be in ourselves.

But what does this mean? When did this happen? When were we crucified? The Bible gives the answer in Galatians 2:19-20: "I have been crucified with Christ. It is no longer I who live, but Christ who lives in me. And the life I now live in the flesh I live by faith in the Son of God, who loved me and gave himself for me." When Christ died, we died. The glorious meaning of the death of Christ is that when he died, all those who are his died in him. The death that he died for us all becomes our death when we are united to Christ by faith (Romans 6:5).

But you say, "Aren't I alive? I feel alive." Well, here is a need for education. We must learn what happened to us. We must be taught these things. That is why Galatians 2:20 and Galatians 6:14 are in the Bible. God is teaching us what happened to us, so that we can know ourselves, and know his way of working with us, and exult in him and in his Son and in the cross as we ought.

LINKING WITH THE DEATH AND LIFE OF CHRIST CRUCIFIED

Consider Galatians 2:19-20 again. We will see that, yes, we are dead and, yes, we are alive. "I have been crucified with Christ [so I am dead]. It is no longer I who live, but Christ who lives in me. And the life I now live in the flesh [so, yes, I am alive, but it isn't the same "I" as the "I" who died] I live by faith in the Son of God, who loved me and gave himself for me." In other words, the "I" who lives is the new "I" of faith. The new creation lives. The believer lives. The old self died on the cross with Jesus.

You may ask, "What's the key for linking up with this reality? How can this be mine? How can I be among the dead who are alive with Christ and who see and savor and spread the glory of the cross?" The answer is implied in the words about *faith* in Galatians 2:20. "The life I now live . . . I live *by faith* in the Son of God." That is the link. God links you to his Son by faith. And when he does, there is a union with the Son of God so that his death becomes your death and his life becomes your life.

DYING, LIVING, AND BOASTING IN THE CROSS

Now let's take all that over to Galatians 6:14, and we will see how we come to live totally for the glory of Christ crucified. "Far be it from me to boast except in the cross of our Lord Jesus Christ, by which the world has been crucified to me, and I to the world." That is, don't boast in anything except in the cross. How shall we become so radically cross-exalting? How can we become the kind of people who trace all our joy back to joy in Christ and him crucified? Answer: The old self that loves to boast and exult and rejoice in other things died. By faith we are united to Christ. His death becomes the death of our self-exalting life. We are raised with him to newness of life. What lives is a new creature whose single passion is to exalt Christ and his cross.

To put it another way, when you put your trust in Christ, your bondage to the world and its overpowering lure is broken. You are a corpse to the world, and the world is a corpse to you. Or to put it positively, according to verse 15, you are a "new creation." The old "you" is dead. A new "you" is alive. And the new you is the you of faith. And what faith does is boast *not* in the world, but in Christ, especially Christ crucified.

This is how you become so cross-centered that you say with Paul, "I will not boast, except in the cross of our Lord Jesus Christ." The world is no longer our treasure. It's not the source of our life or our satisfaction or our joy. Christ is.

SHALL WE PRIZE WHAT HE PRESENTS OR WHAT IT PORTRAYS OF HIM?

But what about safety in the car accident? What about the insurance payment we received? Didn't I say I was happy about that? Isn't that worldly? So am I really dead to the world? Dead to insurance payments and new cars?

I pray that I am dead in the right way. I believe that I am. Not perfectly, I am sure, but in a real sense. How can this be? If I feel glad about safety or health or any good thing, and if these things are things of the world (which they are), then am I dead to the world? Yes, because being dead to the world does not mean having no feelings about the world (see 1 John 2:15; 1 Timothy 4:3). It means that every legitimate pleasure in the world becomes a blood-bought evidence of Christ's love, and an occasion of boasting in the cross. We are dead to insurance payments when the money is not what satisfies, but Christ crucified, the Giver, satisfies.

C. S. Lewis illustrates what I mean by an experience he had in a toolshed.

> I was standing today in the dark toolshed. The sun was shining outside and through the crack at the top of the door there came a sunbeam. From where I stood that beam of light, with the specks of dust floating in it, was the most striking thing in the place. Everything else was almost pitch-black. I was seeing the beam, not seeing things by it.
>
> Then I moved, so that the beam fell on my eyes. Instantly the whole previous picture vanished. I saw no toolshed, and (above all) no beam. Instead I saw, framed in the irregular cranny at the top of the door, green leaves moving on the branches of a tree outside and beyond that, ninety-odd million miles away, the sun. Looking along the beam, and looking at the beam are very different experiences.[2]

The sunbeams of blessing in our lives are bright in and of themselves. They also give light to the ground where we walk. But there is a higher purpose for these blessings. God means for us to do more than stand outside them and admire them for what they are. Even more, he means for us to walk into them and see the sun from which they come. If the beams are beautiful, the sun is even more beautiful. God's aim is not that we merely admire his gifts, but, even more, his glory.

WE DIE TO THE INNOCENT WORLD IN THE BLAZE OF CHRIST'S GLORY

Now the point is that the glory of Christ, manifest especially in his death and resurrection, is the glory above and behind every blessing we enjoy. He purchased everything that is good for us. His glory is where the quest of our affections must end. Everything else is a pointer—a parable of this beauty. When our hearts run back up along the beam of blessing to the source in the blazing glory of the cross, then the worldliness of the blessing is dead, and Christ crucified is everything.

THE ONLY GOD-GLORIFYING LIFE

This is no different than the goal of magnifying the glory of God that we saw in Chapter 2. Christ is the glory of God. His blood-soaked cross is the blazing center of that glory. By it he bought for us every blessing—temporal and eternal. And we don't deserve any. He bought them all. Because of Christ's cross, God's elect are destined to be sons of God. Because of his cross, the wrath of God is taken away. Because of his cross all guilt is removed, and sins are forgiven, and perfect righteousness is imputed to us, and the love of God is poured out in our hearts by the Spirit, and we are being conformed to the image of Christ.

Therefore every enjoyment in this life and the next that is not idolatry is a tribute to the infinite value of the cross of Christ—the burning center of the glory of God. And thus a cross-centered, cross-exalting, cross-saturated life is a God-glorifying life—the *only* God-glorifying life. All others are wasted.

NOTES

1   See http://www.268generation.com/268generation/268declaration.htm [accessed 3-15-03].

2   C. S. Lewis, "Meditation in a Toolshed," in *C. S. Lewis: Essay Collection and Other Short Pieces* (London: Harper Collins, 2000), 607.

CHAPTER 4
MAGNIFYING CHRIST THROUGH PAIN AND DEATH

*L*iving to magnify Christ is costly. This is not surprising. He was crucified. He was treated like a devil. And he calls us to follow him. "If anyone would come after me, let him deny himself and take up his cross and follow me" (Mark 8:34). He says it will probably not go better for us than for him. "If they have called the master of the house Beelzebul,[1] how much more will they malign those of his household" (Matthew 10:25).

But suffering with Jesus on the Calvary road of love is not merely the *result* of magnifying Christ; it is also the *means*. He is made supreme when we are so satisfied in him that we can "let goods and kindred go, this mortal life also" and suffer for the sake of love. His beauty shines most brightly when treasured above health and wealth and life itself. Jesus knew this. He knew that suffering (whether small discomforts or dreadful torture) would be the path in this age for making him most visibly supreme. That is why he calls us to this. He loves us. And love does not mean making much of us or making life easy. It means making us able to enjoy making much of him forever—no matter what it costs.

WE BOAST BEST IN THE CROSS WHEN WE BEAR IT

And it costs us dearly. The normal Christian life is one that boasts only in the cross—the blazing center of God's glory—and does it while bearing the cross. "Whoever does not bear his own cross and come after me cannot be my disciple" (Luke 14:27). Bearing the cross is the means by which we are increasingly liberated to boast in the cross. Suffering is God's design in this sin-soaked world (Romans 8:20). It portrays sin's horror for the world to see. It punishes sin's guilt for those who do not believe in Christ. It breaks sin's power for those who take up their cross and follow Jesus. And because sin is the belittling of the all-satisfying glory of God, the suffering that breaks its power is a severe mercy.

Whatever makes us more and more able to enjoy making much of God is a mercy. For there is no greater joy than joy in the greatness of God. And if we must suffer to see this and savor it most deeply, then suffering is a mercy. And Christ's call to take up our cross and join him on the Calvary road is love.

BONHOEFFER'S RADICAL BOOK FOR MY GENERATION

Dietrich Bonhoeffer was a gift to my generation of students. I pray that his costly message will be rediscovered in each generation. Even though he died at the age of thirty-nine, his life was not wasted. His life and death continue to speak with power. He was hanged in the concentration camp at Flossenbürg, Germany, on April 9, 1945. He had been a pastor and teacher and leader of a small training school for the confessing church and had participated in the Protestant resistance movement against the Nazis.

The book that set fire to the faith of thousands in my generation was called *The Cost of Discipleship*. I read it on Christmas break during my senior year in college. Probably the most famous and life-shaping sentence in the book was, "The cross is not the terrible end to an otherwise God-fearing and happy life, but it meets us at the beginning of our communion with Christ. When Christ calls a man, he bids him come and die."[2] Fleeing from death is the shortest path to a wasted life.

Bonhoeffer's book was a massive indictment of the "cheap grace" that he saw in the Christian Church on both sides of the Atlantic. He believed in justification by grace through faith. But he did not believe that the faith that justifies could ever leave people unchanged by the radical Christ they claim to believe. That was a cheap response to the Gospel. "The only man," he said, "who has the right to say that he is justified by grace alone is the man who has left all to follow Christ."[3]

THE CHRIST-EXALTING PARADOXES OF LIFE

A life devoted to making much of Christ is costly. And the cost is both a consequence and a means of making much of him. If we do not embrace the path of joy-laden, painful love, we will waste our lives. If we do not learn with Paul the Christ-exalting paradoxes of life, we will squander our days pursuing bubbles that burst. He lived "as sorrowful, yet always rejoicing; as poor, yet making many rich; as having nothing, yet possessing everything" (2 Corinthians 6:10). The Calvary road is costly and painful, but it is not joyless.

When we embrace with joy the cost of following Christ, his worth will shine in the world. The cost itself will become a means of making Christ look great. The apostle Paul had one great passion in life. We have seen him say it several ways: to know nothing but Christ and him crucified (1 Corinthians 2:2); to boast only in the cross (Galatians 6:14).

PAUL'S SINGLE PASSION IN LIFE AND DEATH

He talked about his great passion another way that shows us how the cost of making much of Christ is also the means. He said to the Philippian church, "It is my eager expectation and hope that I will not be at all ashamed, but that with full courage now as always Christ will be honored in my body, whether by life or by death. For to me to live is Christ, and to die is gain" (Philippians 1:20-21). Here the question is raised and answered: How do you honor Christ by death? How can the cost of losing everything in this world be a means of making much of Jesus? Let's listen carefully to Paul. Christ has called us to live for his glory and to die for his glory. If we know how to die well, we will know how to live well. This text shows both.

Again we see Paul's single passion in life—"that . . . Christ will be honored in my body, whether by life or by death." If Christ is not made much of in our lives, they are wasted. We exist to make him appear in the world as what he really is—magnificent. If our life and death do not show the worth and wonder of Jesus, they are wasted. This is why Paul said that his aim in life and death was "that . . . Christ . . . be honored."

OUR SHAME AND OUR TREASURE

Notice the unusual way he makes this clear in verse 20: "It is my eager expectation and hope that I will not be at all *ashamed*." Stop here just a moment. Shame is that horrible feeling of guilt or failure when you don't measure up before people whose approval you want very much. It's what the little child feels in the Christmas program when he forgets his lines, and the tears well up, and the silence seems eternal, and the other kids snicker brutally. I remember these horrible times. Or shame is what a president feels when the secret tapes are finally played, and the foul language and all the deceit emerges, and he stands disgraced and guilty before the people.

What then is the opposite of shame? It's when the child remembers the lines and hears the applause. It's when the president governs well and is reelected. The opposite of being shamed is being honored. Yes, usually. But Paul was a very unusual person. And Christians ought to be very unusual people. For Paul, the opposite of being shamed was not *his* being honored, but *Christ's* being honored through him. "It is my eager expectation and hope that I will not be at all ashamed, but that . . . Christ will be honored in my body."

What you love determines what you feel shame about. If you love for men to make much of you, you will feel shame when they don't. But if you love for men to make much of Christ, then you will feel shame if he is belittled on your account. And Paul loved Christ more than he loved anything or anyone. "Whatever gain I had, I counted as loss for the sake of Christ. Indeed, I count everything as loss because of the surpassing worth of knowing Christ Jesus my Lord" (Philippians 3:7-8).

Whenever something is of tremendous value to you, and you cherish its beauty or power or uniqueness, you want to draw others' attention to it and waken in them the same joy. That is why Paul's all-consuming goal in life was for Christ to be magnified. Christ was of infinite value to Paul, and so Paul longed for others to see and savor this value. That is what it means to magnify Christ—to show the magnitude of his value.

DOESN'T DEATH MAKE MAGNIFYING GOD IMPOSSIBLE?

But what if someone objected to Paul at this point and said, "Paul, we see how valuable Christ is to you now—how you enjoy his fellowship, how he gives you a fruitful ministry and delivers your life from spiritual shipwreck. But what will all that mean in the hour of death? Where is the value of Christ then?

If being a Christian costs you your life, how will that help you make much of Christ? Won't that rob you of the very life that can magnify him?"

So Paul adds at the end of verse 20 that his eager expectation is that "Christ will be honored in my body, whether by life *or by death*." Death is a threat to the degree that it frustrates your main goals. Death is fearful to the degree that it threatens to rob you of what you treasure most. But Paul treasured Christ most, and his goal was to magnify Christ. And he saw death not as a frustration of that goal but as an occasion for its fulfillment.

Life and death! They seem like complete opposites—at great enmity with each other. But for Paul—and for all who share his faith—there is a unity, because the same great passion is fulfilled in both—namely, that Christ be magnified in this body—our bodies—whether by life or by death.

In Philippians 1:21, Paul gives a packed summary statement explaining how he is so hopeful that Christ will be magnified in his living and in his dying: "For to me to live is Christ, and to die is gain." Then in verses 22-26 Paul explains both halves of this statement so we can see in more detail how Christ is magnified by life and by death.

Let's take these one at a time.

PAUL'S DISCOVERY OF PETER'S SECRET

First, "For me . . . to die is gain." I wonder if Paul in his conversations with Peter in Jerusalem had talked about dying? I wonder if Peter told him about that experience recorded in John 21 when Jesus, after his resurrection, said to Peter, "When you were young, you used to dress yourself and walk wherever you wanted, but when you are old, you will stretch out your hands, and another will dress you and carry you where you do not want to go" (John 21:18). Then John adds this explanation in his Gospel: "This [Jesus] said to show *by what kind of death [Peter] was to glorify God*" (John 21:19). God had decreed that Peter would make God look great in his dying. I don't doubt that when Peter and Paul gave each other the right hand of fellowship, the manly grip of their hands and the meeting of their eyes communicated this one common passion: to magnify Christ crucified—the blazing center of the glory of God—even in death.

But how are we to magnify Christ in death? Or to put it another way: How can we die so that in our dying the surpassing value of Christ, the magnitude of his worth, becomes visible? Paul's answer here in Philippians 1 is found first in the connection between verse 20 and verse 21. These verses are connected by the word "for" or "because." Boil it down to the words about death: "My eager expectation is that Christ be honored in my body by death, for to me to die is gain." In other words, if you experience death as gain, you magnify Christ in death.

HOW IS DYING GAIN?

Why is that? Verse 23 shows why dying is gain for Paul: "My desire is to depart [that is, to die] and be with Christ, for that is far better." That is what death does: It takes us into more intimacy with Christ. We depart, and we are with Christ, and that, Paul says, is gain. And when you experience death this way, Paul says, you exalt Christ. Experiencing Christ as gain in your dying magnifies Christ. It is "far better" than living here.

Really? Better than all the friends at school? Better than falling in love? Better than hugging your children? Better than professional success? Better than retirement and grandchildren? Yes. A thousand times better. When I preached my candidating sermon for the pastoral position I hold now, this passage of Scripture was my text. That was January 27, 1980. I wanted to show the people from Scripture the single, all-embracing passion of my life—to magnify Christ in all things whether by life or death.

At this point in the message, the question arose: Is death better than life? Is departing to be with Christ better than staying here? I said to them:

> If I didn't believe that, how could I dare to aspire to the role of pastor—anywhere—not to mention at Bethlehem Baptist Church where 108 members are over 80 years old and another 171 over 65? But I do believe it, and say to every gray-haired believer in this church, with all the authority of Christ's apostle, the best is yet to come! And I don't mean a fat pension and a luxury condominium. I mean Christ.[4]

I averaged one funeral every three weeks for the first year and a half of my ministry. And many more after that. It was a sobering and sweetening season for a young pastor. It knit my heart together with many families as we bade *farewell* to friend after friend. And *faring well* is exactly what we believed they did.

IF WE LEARN TO DIE WELL, WE WILL LIVE WELL

What we have learned from Philippians 1 so far is that death (whether by natural causes or by persecution) is a means of making much of Christ. If we suffer or die on the Calvary road of obedience with Christ, the cost of following him is not just a *result* of making much of him, but a *means*. Death makes visible where our treasure is. The way we die reveals the worth of Christ in our hearts. Christ is magnified in my death when I am satisfied with him in my dying—when I experience death as gain because I gain him. Or to say it another way: The essence of praising Christ is prizing Christ. Christ will be praised in my death, if in my death he is prized above life.

Jesus said, "Whoever loves father or mother more than me

is not worthy of me, and whoever loves son or daughter more than me is not worthy of me" (Matthew 10:37). When the hour comes for everything to be taken from us but Christ, we will magnify him by saying, "In him I have everything and more. To die is gain."

If we learn to die like this, we will be ready to live. And if we don't, we will waste our lives. Most of us have some years to live before we go to be with Christ. Even the oldest among us must ask the question, "If we love Christ, how can he be magnified in my behavior this afternoon, this evening, this week?" So we turn to the other half of Philippians 1:21: "To me to live is Christ."

TO LIVE IS CHRIST

What does Paul mean: "To live is Christ"? He begins his explanation in verse 22: "If I am to live in the flesh, that means fruitful labor for me." But that is a strange explanation: "To live is Christ" becomes "To live is fruitful labor for me." What is the fruit that comes from Paul's work? And how is "to live . . . Christ"? The answers come in verses 24-26.

In verse 22 Paul has said, "If I am to live in the flesh, that means fruitful labor for me. Yet which I shall choose I cannot tell." Now in verse 24 he says, "To remain in the flesh is more necessary on your account." So evidently the fruit that Paul's life produces is not only for himself but is very needful for the sake of the Philippian believers. So the phrase, "For me to live is Christ" now becomes "For me to live is to produce fruit that you all need very much." Then verse 25 tells us what this fruit is that the church needs and that Paul's life will produce: "I know that I will remain and continue with you all, for your progress and joy in the faith." So we can see Paul gradually clarifying what he means by "For me to live is Christ."

First, it means: My life is dedicated to producing fruit (verse 22). Second, it means: My life is devoted to producing a fruit that is very necessary for you to have (verse 24). Third, it means: My life is devoted to increasing your faith and helping it to overflow with joy (verse 25).

Now the crucial question is: Why in Paul's mind is it one and the same thing to say on the one hand, "For me to live is Christ," and to say on the other hand, "My life is devoted to your progress and joy in the faith"? I think those two statements are virtually synonymous for Paul in this context.

I LIVE FOR YOUR PROGRESS AND JOY IN FAITH

To see this we need a definition of faith. Ordinarily faith would mean trust or confidence you put in someone who has given good evidence of his reliability and willingness and ability to provide what you need. But when Jesus Christ is the object of faith there is a twist. He himself is what we need. If we only trust Christ to give us gifts and not himself as the all-satisfying gift, then we do not trust him in a way that honors him as our treasure. We simply honor the gifts. *They* are what we really want, not him. So biblical faith in Jesus must mean that we trust him to give us what we need most—namely, himself. That means that faith itself must include at its essence a treasuring of Christ above all things.

Now we are in a position to see why Paul's two aims for his life are in fact one. According to verse 20, his aim is *to magnify Christ in life*; and according to verse 25, his aim is *to promote the progress and joy in the Philippians' faith*. That is why he believes God might let him live. This would be his life: to labor for their "progress and joy in the faith."

But now we have seen that faith is essentially treasuring Christ. The word "joy" in verse 25 ("for your . . . joy in the faith") signals that this treasuring is a joyful treasuring. And if Christ is joyfully treasured, he is magnified. That is the single, all-embracing passion of Paul's life. In other words, Paul is saying, "My life is devoted to producing in you that one great experience of the heart by which Christ is magnified—namely, being satisfied in him, joyfully treasuring him above all else. That's what I mean when I say, 'For me to live is Christ.' That is, for me to live is your Christ-magnifying faith."

THE CHRISTIAN LIFE IS MANY DEATHS

It would be a great mistake at this point if we separated the way death honors Christ from the way life honors Christ. The reason this would be a mistake is that the life of a Christian includes many deaths. Paul said, "I die every day!" (1 Corinthians 15:31). Jesus said, "If anyone would come after me, let him deny himself and take up his cross *daily* and follow me" (Luke 9:23). Daily Christian living is daily Christian dying. The dying I have in mind is the dying of comfort and security and reputation and health and family and friends and wealth and homeland. These may be taken from us at any time in the path of Christ-exalting obedience. To die daily the way Paul did, and to take up our cross daily the way Jesus commanded, is to embrace this life of loss for Christ's sake and count it gain.

In other words, the way we honor Christ in death is to treasure Jesus above the gift of life, and the way we honor Christ in life is to treasure Jesus above life's gifts. This is why Paul used the same word "gain" in relation to Christ at death and in relation to Christ in life. Not only did he say, "To die is *gain*," but he also said, "Whatever *gain* I had [in life!], I counted as loss for the sake of Christ. Indeed, I count everything as loss because of the surpassing worth of knowing Christ Jesus my Lord. For his sake I have suffered the loss of all things and count them as rubbish, in order that I may *gain* Christ" (Philippians 3:7-8).

PAIN AND PLEASURE AS WAYS TO MAKE MUCH OF CHRIST

All of life for the Christian is meant to magnify Christ. This can happen through pleasure, and it can happen through pain. We are focusing here on the pain. The reason for this is not that a thousand pleasant things don't come our way as Christians. Nor is it that we should not enjoy them as gifts of God and glorify him with thanksgiving. We should. That is what the Bible teaches. "Everything created by God is good, and nothing is to be rejected if it is received with thanksgiving, for it is made holy by the word of God and prayer" (1 Timothy 4:4-5). And it is true that "The one who offers thanksgiving as his sacrifice glorifies me" (Psalm 50:23).

The reason I don't stress this is that we are spring-loaded to see the pleasant side of truth. We are fallen, comfort-loving creatures. We are always on the lookout for ways to justify our self-protecting, self-securing, self-pleasing ways of life. I know this about myself. And I am glad that this is not all bad. God "richly supplies us with everything to enjoy" (1 Timothy 6:17).

HOW WE HANDLE LOSS SHOWS WHO OUR TREASURE IS

But what I know even more surely is that the greatest joy in God comes from giving his gifts away, not in hoarding them for ourselves. It is good to work and have. It is better to work and have in order to give. God's glory shines more brightly when he satisfies us in times of loss than when he provides for us in times of plenty. The health, wealth, and prosperity "gospel" swallows up the beauty of Christ in the beauty of his gifts and turns the gifts into idols. The world is not impressed when Christians get rich and say thanks to God. They are impressed when God is so satisfying that we give our riches away for Christ's sake and count it gain.

No one ever said that they learned their deepest lessons of life, or had their sweetest encounters with God, on the sunny days. People go deep with God when the drought comes. That is the way God designed it. Christ aims to be magnified in life most clearly by the way we experience him in our losses. Paul is our example: "We were so utterly burdened beyond our strength that we despaired of life itself. Indeed, we felt that we had received the sentence of death. But that was to make us rely not on ourselves but on God who raises the dead" (2 Corinthians 1:8-9). The design of Paul's suffering was to make radically clear for his own soul, and for ours, that God and God alone is the only treasure who lasts. When everything in life is stripped away except God, and we trust him more because of it, this is gain, and he is glorified.

WASTING LIFE BY RUNNING FROM PAIN

This design for the Christian life is so crucial that we should open our eyes to see how extensively the Bible speaks about it. Untold numbers of professing Christians waste their lives trying to escape the cost of love. They do not see that it is always worth it. There is more of God's glory to be seen and savored through suffering than through self-serving escape. Paul puts it like this: "Though our outer nature is wasting away, our inner nature is being renewed day by day. For this slight momentary affliction is preparing for us an eternal weight of glory beyond all comparison" (2 Corinthians 4:16-17). "Momentary" refers to a lifetime in comparison with eternity. "Slight" refers to suffering and death compared to the weight of everlasting joy in the presence of God. This is what we gain if hold fast to Christ. This is what we waste if we don't.

God designs that tribulations intensify our hope for the

glory of God. Paul says in Romans 5:2 that we have access by faith into grace and "rejoice in hope of the glory of God." Then he tells us in the next two verses how that hope is preserved and sweetened: "More than that, we rejoice in our sufferings, knowing that suffering produces endurance, and endurance produces character, and character produces *hope*" (verses 3-4). This hope that grows and deepens and satisfies through suffering is the hope of verse 2, the "hope of the glory of God." We were made to see and savor this glory. And God, in love, will use whatever trials are necessary to intensify our savoring of his glory.

THERE IS A DIFFERENCE BETWEEN SACRIFICE AND SUICIDE

It is not wrong to pray for healing, to take medicine, to put locks on your doors, to flee unruly mobs. The Bible does not call for suicide. It is presumption to jump off the temple while quoting Scripture promises that God will catch you. God finally decides whether and when the path of obedience will lead to suffering. Satan has his place. He loves to make us miserable and tries to destroy our faith. But God is sovereign over Satan, and all of Satan's aims to destroy the saints are designed by God for the good of his people and the glory of his name.

So it is right to flee, and it is right to stay. One may escape, and one may endure hardship. When to flee and when to stay is an agonizing question for many missionaries and urban workers and Christians in secular workplaces with great opportunity and great conflict. One person who thought more about it than most of us was John Bunyan, the pastor who spent twelve years in prison and wrote *Pilgrim's Progress*. He could have been released from prison if he had agreed not to preach. His wife and children needed him. One of his daughters was blind. It was an agonizing decision. "The parting with my wife and poor children hath often been to me in this place as the pulling of the Flesh from my bones."[5]

Here is what he wrote about the Christian's freedom to stay or flee from danger.

> May we try to escape? Thou mayest do in this as it is in thy heart. If it is in thy heart to fly, fly: if it be in thy heart to stand, stand. Any thing but a denial of the truth. He that flies, has warrant to do so; he that stands, has warrant to do so. Yea, the same man may both fly and stand, as the call and working of God with his heart may be. Moses fled, Exodus 2:15; Moses stood, Hebrews 11:27. David fled, 1 Samuel 19:12; David stood, 1 Samuel 24:8. Jeremiah fled, Jeremiah 37:11-12; Jeremiah stood, Jeremiah 38:17. Christ withdrew himself, Luke 9:10; Christ stood, John 18:1-8. Paul fled, 2 Corinthians 11:33; Paul stood, Act 20:22-23. . . .
>
> There are few rules in this case. The man himself is best able to judge concerning his present strength, and what weight this or that argument has upon his heart to stand or fly. . . . Do not fly out of a slavish fear, but rather because flying is an ordinance of God, opening a door for the escape of some, which door is opened by God's providence, and the escape countenanced by God's Word. Matthew 10:23. . . . If, therefore, when thou hast fled, thou art taken, be not offended at God or man: not at God, for thou art his servant, thy life and thy all are his; not at man, for he is but God's rod, and is ordained, in this, to do thee good. Hast thou escaped? Laugh. Art thou taken? Laugh. I mean, be pleased which way soever things shall go, for that the scales are still in God's hand.[6]

THE PROMISE AND DESIGN OF GOD

But when all is said and done, the *promise* and *design* of God for people who do not waste their lives is clear. "All who desire to live a godly life in Christ Jesus will be persecuted" (2 Timothy

3:12). And when persecution pauses, the groanings of this age remain. "We ourselves, who have the firstfruits of the Spirit, groan inwardly as we wait eagerly for adoption as sons, the redemption of our bodies" (Romans 8:23). We will groan one way or the other. As Paul said, "sorrowful, yet always rejoicing" (2 Corinthians 6:10).

That is the promise. Here's the design. Jesus said to Paul in pain—and to all of us who treasure *him* more than pain-free living—"My grace is sufficient for you, for my power is made perfect in weakness" (2 Corinthians 12:8). Many professing Christians would get angry at this design. They might even scream, "I don't care about your power being perfected! I am in pain! If you love me, get me out of this!" That was not Paul's response. Paul had learned what love is. Love is not Christ's making much of us or making life easy. Love is doing what he must do, at great cost to himself (and often to us), to enable us to enjoy making much of him forever. So Paul responds to Christ's design, "Therefore I will boast all the more gladly of my weaknesses, so that the power of Christ may rest upon me. For the sake of Christ, then, I am content with weaknesses, insults, hardships, persecutions, and calamities. For when I am weak, then I am strong" (2 Corinthians 12:9-10).

ALL LASTING JOY IS ON THE CALVARY ROAD

What a tragic waste when people turn away from the Calvary road of love and suffering. All the riches of the glory of God in Christ are on that road. All the sweetest fellowship with Jesus is there. All the treasures of assurance. All the ecstasies of joy. All the clearest sightings of eternity. All the noblest camaraderie. All the humblest affections. All the most tender acts of forgiving kindness. All the deepest discoveries of God's Word. All the most earnest prayers. They are all on the Calvary road where Jesus walks with his people. Take up your cross and follow

Jesus. On this road, and this road alone, life is Christ and death is gain. Life on every other road is wasted.

NOTES

1   In the time of Christ this was the name for the prince of demons—that is, Satan or the devil.

2   Dietrich Bonhoeffer, *The Cost of Discipleship* (New York: Macmillan, 1967), 99.

3   Ibid., 55.

4   This sermon is available online at www.desiringGod.org (http://www. desiringgod.org/resourcelibrary/sermons/bydate/1980/1823).

5   John Bunyan, *Grace Abounding to the Chief of Sinners* (Hertfordshire, England: Evangelical Press, 1978), 123.

6   John Bunyan, *Seasonable Counsels, or Advice to Sufferers*, in *The Works of John Bunyan*, Vol. 2, ed. George Offor (Edinburgh: Banner of Truth, 1991, orig., 1854), 726.

CHAPTER 5
RISK IS RIGHT—BETTER TO LOSE YOUR LIFE THAN TO WASTE IT

*I*f our single, all-embracing passion is to make much of Christ in life and death, and if the life that magnifies him most is the life of costly love, then life is risk, and risk is right. To run from it is to waste your life.

WHAT IS RISK?

I define risk very simply as an action that exposes you to the possibility of loss or injury. If you take a risk you can lose money, you can lose face, you can lose your health or even your life. And what's worse, if you take a risk, you may endanger other people and not just yourself. Their lives may be at stake. Will a wise and loving person, then, ever take a risk? Is it wise to expose yourself to loss? Is it loving to endanger others? Is losing life the same as wasting it?

It depends. Of course you can throw your life away in a hundred sinful ways and die as a result. In that case, losing life and wasting it would be the same. But losing life is not always the same as wasting it. What if the circumstances are such that *not* taking a risk will result in loss and injury? It may not be wise to play it safe. And what if a successful risk would bring great benefit to many people, and its failure would bring harm only to yourself? It may not be loving to choose comfort or security when something great may be achieved for the cause of Christ and for the good of others.

RISK IS WOVEN INTO THE FABRIC OF OUR FINITE LIVES

Why is there such a thing as risk? Because there is such a thing as ignorance. If there were no ignorance there would be no risk. Risk is possible because we don't know how things will turn out. This means that God can take no risks.[1] He knows the outcome of all his choices before they happen. This is what it means to be God over against all the gods of the nations (Isaiah 41:23; 42:8-9; 44:6-8; 45:21; 46:8-11; 48:3). And since he knows the outcome of all his actions before they happen, he plans accordingly. His omniscience rules out the very possibility of taking risks.[2]

But not so with us. We are not God; we are ignorant. We don't know what will happen tomorrow. God does not tell us in detail what he intends to do tomorrow or five years from now. Evidently God intends for us to live and act in ignorance and in uncertainty about the outcome of our actions.

He says to us, for example, in James 4:13-15:

> Come now, you who say, "Today or tomorrow we will go into such and such a town and spend a year there and trade and make a profit"—yet you do not know what tomorrow will bring. What is your life? For you are a mist that appears for a little time and then vanishes. Instead you ought to say, "If the Lord wills, we will live and do this or that."

You don't know if your heart will stop before you finish

reading this page. You don't know if some oncoming driver will swerve out of his lane and hit you head-on in the next week, or if the food in the restaurant may have some deadly virus in it, or if a stroke may paralyze you before the week is out, or if some man with a rifle will shoot you at the shopping center. We are not God. We do not know about tomorrow.

EXPLODING THE MYTH OF SAFETY

Therefore risk is woven into the fabric of our finite lives. We cannot avoid risk even if we want to. Ignorance and uncertainty about tomorrow is our native air. All of our plans for tomorrow's activities can be shattered by a thousand unknowns whether we stay at home under the covers or ride the freeways. One of my aims is to explode the myth of safety and to somehow deliver you from the enchantment of security. Because it's a mirage. It doesn't exist. Every direction you turn there are unknowns and things beyond your control.

The tragic hypocrisy is that the enchantment of security lets us take risks every day for ourselves but paralyzes us from taking risks for others on the Calvary road of love. We are deluded and think that it may jeopardize a security that in fact does not even exist. The way I hope to explode the myth of safety and to disenchant you with the mirage of security is simply to go to the Bible and show that it is right to risk for the cause of Christ, and not to is to waste your life.

"MAY THE LORD DO WHAT SEEMS GOOD TO HIM"

Consider the context of 2 Samuel 10. The Amalekites had shamed the messengers of Israel and made themselves odious in the sight of David. To protect themselves they had hired the Syrians to fight with them against the Israelites. Joab, the commander of Israel's forces, found himself surrounded with

Amalekites on one side and Syrians on the other. So he divided his troops, put his brother Abishai in charge of one troop of fighters, and led the other himself.

In verse 11 they pledged to help each other. Then comes this great word in verse 12: "Be of good courage, and let us be courageous for our people, and for the cities of our God, and may the LORD do what seems good to him." What do these last words mean, "May the LORD do what seems good to him"? It means that Joab had made a strategic decision for the cities of God, and he did not know how it would turn out. He had no special revelation from God on this issue. He had to make a decision on the basis of sanctified wisdom. He had to risk or run. He did not know how it would turn out. So he made his decision, and he handed the results over to God. And this was right.

"IF I PERISH, I PERISH"

Queen Esther is another example of courageous risk in the service of love and for the glory of God. There was a Jewish man named Mordecai who lived in the fifth century before Christ during the Jews' exile. He had a younger orphaned cousin named Esther whom he had adopted as a daughter. She grew up to be beautiful and eventually was taken by Persia's King Ahasuerus to be his queen. Haman, one of Ahasuerus's chief princes, hated Mordecai and all the Jewish refugees and persuaded the king to decree that they be exterminated. The king did not realize that his own queen was a Jew.

Mordecai sent word to Esther to go before the king and plead the case of her people. But Esther knew there was a royal law that anyone who approached the king without being called would be put to death, unless he lifted his golden scepter. She also knew that her people's lives were at stake. Esther sent her response to Mordecai with these words:

"Go, gather all the Jews to be found in Susa, and hold a fast on my behalf, and do not eat or drink for three days, night or day. I and my young women will also fast as you do. Then I will go to the king, though it is against the law, and if I perish, I perish." (Esther 4:15-16)

"If I perish, I perish." What does that mean? It means that Esther did not know what the outcome of her act would be. She had no special revelation from God. She made her decision on the basis of wisdom and love for her people and trust in God. She had to risk or run. She did not know how it would turn out. So she made her decision and handed the results over to God. "If I perish, I perish." And this was right.

"WE WILL NOT SERVE YOUR GODS"

Consider one more example from the Old Testament. The setting is Babylon. The Jewish people are in exile. The king is Nebuchadnezzar. He sets up an image of gold, then commands that when the trumpet sounds, all the people will bow down to the image. But Shadrach, Meshach, and Abednego did not bow down. They worshiped the one true God of Israel.

So Nebuchadnezzar threatened them and said that if they did not worship the image, they would be thrown into the fiery furnace. They answered:

O Nebuchadnezzar, we have no need to answer you in this matter. If this be so, our God whom we serve is able to deliver us from the burning fiery furnace, and he will deliver us out of your hand, O king. But if not, be it known to you, O king, that we will not serve your gods or worship the golden image that you have set up. (Daniel 3:16-18)

This was sheer risk. "We believe our God will deliver us. But even if he doesn't, we will not serve your gods." They did not know how it would turn out. They said virtually the same thing Esther said: "If we perish, we perish." And they handed the outcome to God the same way Joab and Abishai did: "And may the LORD do what seems good to him." And this was right. It is right to risk for the cause of God.

"I AM READY TO DIE FOR THE NAME OF THE LORD JESUS"

The great New Testament risk-taker was the apostle Paul. Picture him first on his way to Jerusalem after years of suffering for Christ almost everywhere he went. He had bound himself in the Holy Spirit (Acts 19:21) to go to Jerusalem. He had collected money for the poor, and he was going to see that it was delivered faithfully. He got as far as Caesarea, and a prophet named Agabus came down from Judea, symbolically bound his own hands and feet with Paul's belt, and said, "Thus says the Holy Spirit, 'This is how the Jews at Jerusalem will bind the man who owns this belt and deliver him into the hands of the Gentiles'" (Acts 21:11).

When the believers heard, this they begged Paul not to go to Jerusalem. He responded, "What are you doing, weeping and breaking my heart? For I am ready not only to be imprisoned but even to die in Jerusalem for the name of the Lord Jesus" (Acts 21:13).Then, Luke tells us, his friends relented: "And since he would not be persuaded, we ceased and said, 'Let the will of the Lord be done'" (Acts 21:14).

In other words, Paul believed that this trip to Jerusalem was necessary for the cause of Christ. He did not know the details of what would happen there or what the outcome would be. Arrest and affliction for sure. But then what? Death? Imprisonment? Banishment? No one knew. So what did they say? They could agree on one thing: "The will of the Lord be done!" Or as Joab said, "May the LORD do what seems good to him." And this was right.

"IN EVERY CITY . . . AFFLICTIONS AWAIT ME"

In fact, Paul's whole life was one stressful risk after another. He said in Acts 20:23, "The Holy Spirit testifies to me in every city that imprisonment and afflictions await me." But he never knew in what form they would come, or when they would come, or by whom they would come. Paul had decided to risk his life in Jerusalem with the full knowledge of what it might be like. What he had already endured left him no doubt about what might happen in Jerusalem:

> *Five times I received at the hands of the Jews the forty lashes less one. Three times I was beaten with rods. Once I was stoned. Three times I was shipwrecked; a night and a day I was adrift at sea; on frequent journeys, in danger from rivers, danger from robbers, danger from my own people, danger from Gentiles, danger in the city, danger in the wilderness, danger at sea, danger from false brothers; in toil and hardship, through many a sleepless night, in hunger and thirst, often without food, in cold and exposure. And, apart from other things, there is the daily pressure on me of my anxiety for all the churches. (2 Corinthians 11:24-28)*

What does this mean? It means that Paul never knew where the next blow would come from. Every day he risked his life for the cause of God. The roads weren't safe. The rivers weren't safe. His own people, the Jews, weren't safe. The Gentiles weren't safe. The cities weren't safe. The wilderness wasn't safe. The sea wasn't safe. Even the so-called Christian brothers weren't safe. Safety was a mirage. It didn't exist for the apostle Paul.

He had two choices: waste his life or live with risk. And he answered this choice clearly: "But I do not account my life of any value nor as precious to myself, if only I may finish my course and the ministry that I received from the Lord Jesus, to testify to the gospel of the grace of God" (Acts 20:24). He never knew what the day would hold. But the Calvary road beckoned. And he risked his life every day. And this was right.

"IF THEY PERSECUTED ME, THEY WILL ALSO PERSECUTE YOU"

Lest we think that this risk-taking life was unique to Paul, he made it a point to tell young Christians that they would meet unspecified troubles. After establishing new churches on his first missionary journey, he returned some months later "strengthening the souls of the disciples, encouraging them to continue in the faith, and saying that *through many tribulations we must enter the kingdom of God*" (Acts 14:22). When he wrote to the young Thessalonian church, he expressed concern that they might have been shaken by their afflictions and said to them, "You yourselves know that we have been destined for this [that is, for these afflictions]" (1 Thessalonians 3:3). In other words, the Christian life is a call to risk.

Jesus had made this clear. He said, for example, in Luke 21:16, "You will be delivered up even by parents and brothers and relatives and friends, and some of you they will put to death." The key word here is *some*. "Some of you they will put to death." This word puts the earthly life of the disciples in great uncertainty. Not all will die for the cause of Christ. But not all will live either. Some will die. And some will live. This is what I mean by risk. It is the will of God that we be uncertain about how life on this earth will turn out for us. And therefore it is the will of the Lord that we take risks for the cause of God.

Life was hard for Jesus, and he said it would be hard for his followers. "Remember the word that I said to you: 'A servant is not greater than his master.' If they persecuted me, they will also persecute you" (John 15:20). So Peter warned the churches of Asia that mistreatment would be normal. "Beloved, do not be surprised at the fiery trial when it comes upon you to test you, as though something strange were happening to you. But rejoice insofar as you share Christ's sufferings, that you may also rejoice and be glad when his glory is revealed. If you are insulted for the name of Christ, you are blessed, because the Spirit of glory and of God rests upon you" (1 Peter 4:12-14).

TO BECOME A CHRISTIAN WAS TO RISK YOUR LIFE

The first three centuries of the Christian church set the pattern of growth under threat. Stephen Neill, in his *History of Christian Missions*, wrote, "Undoubtedly, Christians under the Roman Empire had no legal right to existence, and were liable to the utmost stringency of the law. . . . Every Christian knew that sooner or later he might have to testify to his faith at the cost of his life."[3] Might. There's the risk. It was always there. Maybe we will be killed for being Christians. Maybe we won't. It is a risk. That was normal. And to become a Christian under those circumstances was right.

In fact, it was the Christ-exalting love that the Christians showed in spite of risk that stunned the pagan world. The Roman Emperor Julian (A.D. 332-363) wanted to breathe new life into the ancient pagan religion but saw more and more people drawn to Christianity. He wrote with frustration against these "atheists" (who did not believe in the Roman gods, but in Christ):

> Atheism [i.e., Christian faith] has been specially advanced through the loving service rendered to strangers, and through their care for the burial of the dead. It is a scandal there is not a single Jew who is a beggar, and that the godless Galileans care not only for their own poor but for ours as well; while those who belong to us look in vain for the help that we should render them.[4]

It is costly to follow Christ. There is risk everywhere. But, as we saw in Chapter 3, this very risk is the means by which the value of Christ shines more brightly.

HOW TO WASTE FORTY YEARS AND THOUSANDS OF LIVES

But what happens when the people of God do not escape from the beguiling enchantment of security? What happens if they try to live their lives in the mirage of safety? The answer is wasted lives. Do you remember the time it happened?

It had been less than three years since the people of Israel came out of Egypt by the power of God. Now they were on the borders of the Promised Land. The Lord said to Moses, "Send men to spy out the land of Canaan, which I am giving to the people of Israel" (Numbers 13:2). So Moses sent Caleb, Joshua, and ten other men. After forty days they returned with a huge cluster of grapes hung on a pole between two men. Caleb issued the hope-filled call to his people: "Let us go up at once and occupy it, for we are well able to overcome it" (Numbers 13:30). But the others said, "We are not able to go up against the people, for they are stronger than we are" (v. 31).

Caleb was unable to explode the myth of safety. The people were gripped by the beguiling enchantment of security—the notion that there is a sheltered way of life apart from the path of God-exalting obedience. They murmured against Moses and Aaron and decided to go back to Egypt—the great mirage of safety.

Joshua tried to free them from their stupor.

> The land, which we passed through to spy it out, is an exceedingly good land. If the LORD delights in us, he will bring us into this land and give it to us, a land that flows with milk and honey. Only do not rebel against the LORD.

And do not fear the people of the land, for they are bread for us. Their protection is removed from them, and the LORD *is with us; do not fear them. (Numbers 14:7-9)*

But not even Joshua could explode the myth of safety. The people were drunk in a dreamworld of security. And they tried to stone Caleb and Joshua. The result was thousands of wasted lives and wasted years. It was clearly wrong not to take the risk of battling the giants in the land of Canaan. Oh, how much is wasted when we do not risk for the cause of God!

WHAT ABOUT YOU?

Risk is right. And the reason is not because God promises success to all our ventures in his cause. There is no promise that every effort for the cause of God will succeed, at least not in the short run. John the Baptist risked calling King Herod an adulterer when he divorced his own wife in order to take his brother's wife. For this John got his head chopped off. And he had done right to risk his life for the cause of God and truth. Jesus had no criticism for him, only the highest praise (Matthew 11:11).

Paul risked going up to Jerusalem to complete his ministry to the poor. He was beaten and thrown in prison for two years and then shipped off to Rome and executed there two years later. And he did right to risk his life for the cause of Christ. How many graves are there in Africa and Asia because thousands of young missionaries were freed by the power of the Holy Spirit from the enchantment of security and then risked their lives to make much of Christ among the unreached peoples of the world!

And now what about you? Are you caught in the enchantment of security, paralyzed from taking any risks for the cause of God? Or have you been freed by the power of the Holy Spirit from the mirage of Egyptian safety and comfort? Do you men ever say with Joab, "For the sake of the name, I'll try it! And may the LORD do what seems good to him"? Do you women ever say with Esther, "For the sake of Christ, I'll try it! And if I perish, I perish"?

RISKING FOR THE WRONG REASONS

There is more than one danger in calling Christians to take risks. I mentioned one of them in Chapter 4, namely, that we might become so fixated on self-denial that we are unable to enjoy the proper pleasures of this life that God has given for our good. Another danger, which is worse, is that we might be drawn to a life of risk for self-exalting reasons. We might feel the adrenaline of heroism rising. We might scorn the lazy and cowardly and feel superior. We might think of risk as a kind of righteousness that makes us acceptable to God. What would be missing from all these mistakes is childlike faith in the sovereign rule of God in the world and in his triumphant love.

I have been assuming that the power and the motive behind taking risks for the cause of God is not heroism, or the lust for adventure, or the courage of self-reliance, or the need to earn God's good will, but rather faith in the all-providing, all-ruling, all-satisfying Son of God, Jesus Christ. The strength to risk losing face for the sake of Christ is the faith that God's love will lift up your face in the end and vindicate your cause. The strength to risk losing money for the cause of the Gospel is the faith that we have a treasure in the heavens that cannot fail. The strength to risk losing life in this world is faith in the promise that he who loses his life in this world will save it for the age to come.

This is very different from heroism and self-reliance. When we risk losing face or money or life because we believe God will always help us and use our loss, in the end, to make us more glad in his glory, then it's not we who get the praise because of our courage; it's God who gets the praise because of his care. In this way risk reflects God's value, not our valor.

This foundation for fearlessness must not be assumed. We are wired to risk for the wrong reasons. Without Christ, we are all legalists or lechers at heart—wanting to do our own thing, or wanting to do God's thing in our way to prove our own ability. Since we are wired this way, we need protection. God has given us another way to pursue risk. Do it "by the strength that God supplies—in order that in everything God may be glorified through Jesus Christ" (1 Peter 4:11). And the way God supplies his strength is through faith in his promises. Every loss we risk in order to make much of Christ, God promises to restore a thousandfold with his all-satisfying fellowship.

THE POWER TO RISK IS IN THE PROMISE OF GOD

Earlier in this chapter I mentioned Luke 21:16 where Jesus says to his disciples, "Some of you they will put to death." But I did not mention the promise that follows: "You will be hated by all for my name's sake. *But not a hair of your head will perish*" (verse 18). This is one of those painful paradoxes in the Bible: "Some of you they will put to death. . . . But not a hair of your head will perish"! What does this mean? What is Jesus trying to say to us when he says, "Go ahead and risk obedience; some of you they will put to death; but not a hair of your head will perish"?

I think the best commentary on these verses is Romans 8:35-39.

Who shall separate us from the love of Christ? Shall tribulation, or distress, or persecution, or famine, or nakedness, or danger, or sword? As it is written, "For your sake we are being killed all the day long; we are regarded as sheep to be slaughtered." No, in all these things we are more than conquerors through him who loved us. For I am sure that neither death nor life, nor angels nor rulers, nor things present nor

*things to come, nor powers, nor height nor depth, nor any-
thing else in all creation, will be able to separate us from the
love of God in Christ Jesus our Lord.*

Compare these terrible and wonderful words with what Jesus
said: "Some of you they will put to death. . . . But not a hair of
your head will perish."

Like Jesus, Paul says that the love of Christ for us does not elim-
inate our suffering. On the contrary, our very attachment to Christ
will bring suffering. What is Paul's answer to his own question in
verse 35: "Shall tribulation, or distress, or persecution, or famine,
or nakedness, or danger, or sword separate us from the love of
Christ?" His answer in verse 37 is a resounding NO! But don't
miss the implication of the question: The reason these things will
not separate us from the love of Christ is not because they don't
happen to people whom Christ loves. They do. Paul's quoting of
Psalm 44:22 shows that these things do in fact happen to Christ's
people. "For your sake we are being killed all the day long; we are
regarded as sheep to be slaughtered." In other words, Christ's love
for us does not spare us these sufferings. Risk is real. The Christian
life is a painful life. Not joyless. But not painless either.

DOES GOD REALLY SUPPLY ALL WE NEED?

This is the meaning of the little word "in" found in verse 37:
"*In* all these things we are more than conquerors. . . ." We are
more than conquerors *in* our afflictions, not by avoiding them.
So Paul agrees with Jesus: "Some of you they will put to death."
Obedience is risk. And it is right to risk for the cause of God.
Some of the risks are mentioned in verse 35:

- "tribulation"—the trouble and oppression of various kinds
  that Paul says we must walk through on our way to heaven
  (Acts 14:22).

- "distress"—calamities that bring stress and threaten to break us like a stick (2 Corinthians 6:4; 12:10).
- "persecution"—active opposition from the enemies of the Gospel (Matthew 5:11-12).
- "danger"—every kind of threat or menace to body, soul, and family (2 Corinthians 11:26).
- "sword"—the weapon that killed James (Acts 12:2).
- "famine and nakedness"—the lack of food and clothing.

I put "famine and nakedness" last because they pose the greatest problem. Did not Jesus say:

> Do not be anxious about your life, what you will eat or what you will drink, nor about your body, what you will put on. Is not life more than food, and the body more than clothing? . . . do not be anxious, saying, "What shall we eat?" or "What shall we drink?" or "What shall we wear?" . . . your heavenly Father knows that you need them all. But seek first the kingdom of God and his righteousness, and all these things will be added to you. (Matthew 6:25, 31-33)

"Well, which is it?" we might ask. Are Christians subject to "famine and nakedness" or will God provide "all these things" when we need them? Will Christians never hunger or starve or be ill-clothed? Have not some of the greatest saints in the world been stripped and starved? What about Hebrews 11:37-38? "They were stoned, they were sawn in two, they were killed with the sword. They went about in skins of sheep and goats, destitute, afflicted, mistreated—of whom the world was not worthy—wandering about in deserts and mountains, and in dens and caves of the earth." The losses and miseries of these believers was not owing to their unbelief. They were faithful—people "of whom the world was not worthy."

ALL YOU NEED TO DO HIS WILL AND BE HAPPY FOREVER

What, then, does Jesus mean, "All these things—all your food and clothing—will be added to you when you seek the kingdom of God first"? He means the same thing he meant when he said, "Some of you they will put to death. . . . But not a hair of your head will perish" (Luke 21:16-18). He meant that you will have everything you need to do his will and be eternally and supremely happy in him.

How much food and clothing are necessary? Necessary for what? we must ask. Necessary to be comfortable? No, Jesus did not promise comfort. Necessary to avoid shame? No, Jesus called us to bear shame for his name with joy. Necessary to stay alive? No, he did not promise to spare us death—of any kind. Persecution and plague consume the saints. Christians die on the scaffold, and Christians die of disease. That's why Paul wrote, "We ourselves, who have the firstfruits of the Spirit, groan inwardly as we wait eagerly for adoption as sons, the redemption of our bodies" (Romans 8:23).

What Jesus meant was that our Father in heaven would never let us be tested beyond what we are able (1 Corinthians 10:13). If there is one scrap of bread that you need, as God's child, in order to keep your faith in the dungeon of starvation, you will have it. God does not promise enough food for comfort or life— he promises enough so that you can trust him and do his will.[5]

I CAN DO ALL THINGS THROUGH CHRIST, EVEN STARVE

When Paul promised, "My God will supply every need of yours according to his riches in glory in Christ Jesus," he had just said, "I know how to be brought low, and I know how to abound. In any and every circumstance, I have learned the secret of facing plenty and *hunger*, abundance and *need*. I can do all things through him who strengthens me" (Philippians 4:12-13, 19). "All things" means "I can suffer hunger through him who strengthens me. I can be destitute of food and clothing through him who strengthens me." That is what Jesus promises. He will never leave us or forsake us (Hebrews 13:5). If we starve, he will be our everlasting, life-giving bread. If we are shamed with nakedness, he will be our perfect, all-righteous apparel. If we are tortured and made to scream in our dying pain, he will keep us from cursing his name and will restore our beaten body to everlasting beauty.

THE FAR SIDE OF EVERY RISK, TRIUMPHANT LOVE

The bottom-line comfort and assurance in all our risk-taking for Christ is that nothing will ever separate us from the love of Christ. Paul asks, "Shall tribulation, or distress, or persecution, or famine, or nakedness, or danger, or sword *separate us from the love of Christ?*" (Romans 8:35). His answer is, NO! In other words, no misery that a true Christian ever experiences is evidence that he has been cut off from the love of Christ. The love of Christ triumphs over all misery. Romans 8:38-39 makes this crystal-clear: "For I am sure that neither death nor life, nor angels nor rulers, nor things present nor things to come, nor powers, nor height nor depth, nor anything else in all creation, will be able to separate us from the love of God in Christ Jesus our Lord."

On the far side of every risk—even if it results in death—the love of God triumphs. This is the faith that frees us to risk for the cause of God. It is not heroism, or lust for adventure, or courageous self-reliance, or efforts to earn God's favor. It is childlike faith in the triumph of God's love—that on the other side of all our risks, for the sake of righteousness, God will still be holding us. We will be eternally satisfied in him. Nothing will have been wasted.

HOW CAN IT GET BETTER THAN BEING CONQUERORS?

But there is even more to the promise that sustains us in times of risk for Christ's sake. Paul asks "If God is for us, who can be against us?" (Romans 8:31). The answer he intends us to give is, Nobody. It's the same as saying, "If God is for us, no one can be against us." That seems naïve. It's like saying when your head is cut off, "Not a hair of my head has perished." These excessive statements, it seems, are meant to say more than we have said so far. They intend to say something more than that dying saints won't be separated from Christ.

This "something more" comes out in the words, "more than conquerors." "In all these things we are more than conquerors through him who loved us" (Romans 8:37). What does "more than conquerors" mean? How can you be more than a conqueror when you risk for the cause of God and get hurt for it?

If you venture some act of obedience that magnifies the supreme value of Jesus Christ and get attacked by one of the enemies mentioned in verse 35, say, famine or sword, what must happen for you to be called simply "a conqueror"? Answer: You must not be separated from the love of Jesus Christ. The aim of the attacker is to destroy you, and cut you off from Christ, and bring you to final ruin without God. You are a conqueror if you defeat this aim and remain in the love of Christ. God has promised that this will happen. Trusting this, we risk.

But what must happen in this conflict with famine and sword if you are to be called more than a conqueror? One biblical answer is that a conqueror defeats his enemy, but one who is more than a conqueror subjugates his enemy. A conqueror nullifies the purpose of his enemy; one who is more than a conqueror makes the enemy serve his own purposes. A conqueror strikes down his foe; one who is more than a conqueror makes his foe his slave.

Practically what does this mean? Let's use Paul's own words

in 2 Corinthians 4:17: "This slight momentary affliction is preparing [effecting, or working, or bringing about] for us an eternal weight of glory beyond all comparison." Here we could say that "affliction" is one of the attacking enemies. What has happened in Paul's conflict with it? It has certainly not separated him from the love of Christ. But even more, it has been taken captive, so to speak. It has been enslaved and made to serve Paul's everlasting joy. "Affliction," the former enemy, is now working for Paul. It is preparing for Paul "an eternal weight of glory." His enemy is now his slave. He has not only conquered his enemy. He has more than conquered him.

Affliction raised his sword to cut off the head of Paul's faith. But instead the hand of faith snatched the arm of affliction and forced it to cut off part of Paul's worldliness. Affliction is made the servant of godliness and humility and love. Satan meant it for evil, but God meant it for good. The enemy became Paul's slave and worked for him an even greater weight of glory than he would have ever had without the fight. In that way Paul—and every follower of Christ—is more than a conqueror.

THE ONLY ROAD THAT LEADS TO LASTING JOY

This is the promise that empowers us to take risks for the sake of Christ. It is not the impulse of heroism, or the lust for adventure, or the courage of self-reliance, or the need to earn God's favor. It is simple trust in Christ—that in him God will do everything necessary so that we can enjoy making much of him forever. Every good poised to bless us, and every evil arrayed against us, will in the end help us boast only in the cross, magnify Christ, and glorify our Creator. Faith in these promises frees us to risk and to find in our own experience that it is better to lose our life than to waste it.

Therefore, it is right to risk for the cause of Christ. It is right to engage the enemy and say, "May the LORD do what seems good to him." It is right to serve the people of God, and say, "If I perish, I perish!" It is right to stand before the fiery furnace of affliction and refuse to bow down to the gods of this world. This is the road that leads to fullness of joy and pleasures forevermore. At the end of every other road—secure and risk-free—we will put our face in our hands and say, "I've wasted it!"

NOTES

1   This view is clearly and consciously opposed to the view called open theism which believes that God takes real risks in the sense that he does not know the outcome of many events that he sets in motion. This view is represented, for example, by John Sanders, *The God Who Risks: A Theology of Providence* (Downers Grove, Ill.: InterVarsity Press, 1998) and Gregory A. Boyd, *Satan and the Problem of Evil: Constructing a Trinitarian Warfare Theodicy* (Downers Grove, Ill.: InterVarsity Press, 2001) and is criticized effectively, I believe, by R. K. McGregor Wright, *No Place for Sovereignty: What's Wrong with Freewill Theism?* (Downers Grove, Ill.: InterVarsity Press, 1996); Bruce A. Ware, *God's Lesser Glory: The Diminished God of Open Theism* (Wheaton, Ill.: Crossway Books, 2000); John M. Frame, *No Other God: A Response to Open Theism* (Phillipsburg, N. J.: Presbyterian & Reformed, 2001); and John Piper, Justin Taylor, Paul Kjoss Helseth, eds., *Beyond the Bounds: Open Theism and the Undermining of Biblical Christianity* (Wheaton, Ill.: Crossway Books, 2003).

2   See more on why God cannot be a risk-taker in John Piper, *The Pleasures of God: Meditations on God's Delight in Being God*, 2nd edition (Sisters, Ore.: Multnomah, 2000), 54-62.

3   Stephen Neill, *A History of Christian Missions* (Middlesex, England: Penguin, 1964), 42-43.

4   Ibid., 42.

5   This is the way I would understand the many general promises in the Old Testament to the effect that the needs of the righteous will always be met. For example, Proverbs 10:3, "The LORD does not let the righteous go hungry, but he thwarts the craving of the wicked." I think this is 1) generally true in the way God runs the world—upright, hardworking people prosper and have enough; and 2) always and absolutely true in the sense that the righteous will never hunger beyond what they are able to endure for the sake of Christ. See John Piper, "'No Evil Will Befall You.' Really?" in *A Godward Life, Savoring the Supremacy of God in All of Life, Book Two* (Sisters, Ore.: Multnomah, 1999), 53-55.

CHAPTER 6
THE GOAL OF LIFE—GLADLY MAKING OTHERS GLAD IN GOD

$\mathcal{I}$t is impossible to risk your life to make others glad in God if you are an unforgiving person. If you are wired to see other people's faults and failures and offenses, and treat them roughly, you will not take risks for their joy. This wiring—and it is universal in all human beings—must be dismantled. We will not gladly risk to make people glad in God if we hate them, or hold grudges against them, or are repelled by their faults and foibles. We must become forgiving people.

Don't start raising objections about the hard cases. I am talking about a spirit, not a list of criteria for when we do this or that. Nor am I talking about wimpy grace that can't rebuke or discipline or fight. The question is, do we lean toward mercy? Do we default to grace? Do we have a forgiving spirit? Without it we will walk away from need and waste our lives.

FORGIVENESS IS GOOD BECAUSE IT GIVES US GOD

The biblical motive for being a forgiving person may be deeper than being forgiven. It is true to say: The motive for being a forgiving person is that we have been forgiven by God when we did not deserve it. "Be kind to one another, tenderhearted, forgiving one another, *as God in Christ forgave you*" (Ephesians 4:32). But the bottom of this motive is not God's forgiveness, but what God's forgiveness gives. It gives us God.

Why do we cherish being forgiven by God? There are answers to this question that would dishonor him, because there are benefits from forgiveness that a person may love without loving God. We might say, "I cherish being forgiven by God because I hate the misery of a guilty conscience." Or " . . . because I hate the prospect of pain in hell." Or " . . . because I want to go to heaven to see my loved ones and have a new body with no sickness." Where is God in these reasons for cherishing forgiveness? In the best case he is there in all these reasons as the real treasure of life.

If so, then these delights are really ways of cherishing God himself. A free and clean conscience enables us to see more of God and frees us to enjoy him. Escape from hell at the cost of Christ's blood shows us more of God's commitment to merciful holiness and his desire for our happiness. The gift of seeing loved ones highlights God's wonder in creating relationships of love. Getting a new body deepens our identification with the glorified Christ. But if God himself is not there in these gifts—and I fear he is not for many professing Christians—then we do not know what forgiveness is for.

Forgiveness is essentially God's way of removing the great obstacle to our fellowship with him. By canceling our sin and paying for it with the death of his own Son, God opens the way for us to see him and know him and enjoy him forever. Seeing and savoring him is the goal of forgiveness. Soul-satisfying fellowship with our Father is the aim of the cross. If we love being forgiven for other reasons alone, we are not forgiven, and we will waste our lives.

What, then, is the root motivation for being a forgiving person? "Forgive one another, as God in Christ forgave you." We are to forgive "as God . . . forgave" us. God forgave us in such a way that infinite joy in his fellowship becomes ours. God is the goal of forgiveness. He is also the ground and the means of forgiveness. It comes *from* him; it was accomplished *through* his Son; and it leads people back *to* him with their sins cast into the deepest sea. Therefore the motive for being a forgiving person is the joy of being freely and joyfully at home with God. At great cost to himself God gave us what we needed above all things: himself for our enjoyment forever. God's forgiveness is important for one reason: It gives us God![1]

WHAT FORGIVERS WANT TO GIVE

Our impulse for being forgiving people is the joy we have in a forgiving God. Not just in being forgiven, but in being given joy in God by being forgiven. If we do not see this and experience this, we will probably turn God-centered motives into a kind of benevolence that tries to do good for man without knowing what the greatest good really is—namely, all-satisfying pleasure in God. But if we experience forgiveness as the free and undeserved gift of joy in God, then we will be carried by this joy, with love, into a world of sin and suffering. Our aim there will be that others, through Jesus Christ, will find forgiveness and everlasting joy in God.

Joy in God overflows in glad-hearted mercy to people, because joy in the merciful God cannot spurn being merciful. You cannot despise becoming what you enjoy about God. Joy in the God who did not spare his own Son but gave him up for undeserving sinners cannot return evil for evil. That joy will love being merciful (Micah 6:8). Joy in the God who is slow to anger cannot coexist with its own impatience. It will fight for the triumph of what it admires in God. Joy in the God who spends eternity showing "the immeasurable riches of his grace in kindness toward us" (Ephesians 2:7) delights to be generous and looks for ways to give.

NOT CHRISTIANS BECAUSE THEY DO NOT WANT TO GIVE

Robert Murray M'Cheyne, a Scottish pastor who died at the age of twenty-nine in 1843, spoke of the mercy and generosity of Christians as the evidence that they were indeed Christians. He loved the poor in his parish, and he feared for those who did not look for ways to show them mercy.

> I am concerned for the poor but more for you. I know not what Christ will say to you in the great day. . . . I fear there are many hearing me who may know well that *they are not Christians, because they do not love to give.* To give largely and liberally, not grudging at all, requires a new heart; an old heart would rather part with its life-blood than its money. Oh my friends! Enjoy your money; make the most of it; give none away; enjoy it quickly for I can tell you, you will be beggars throughout eternity.[2]

THE DILEMMA WHERE WE NO LONGER HANG

What is the nature and aim of glad-hearted, Christian giving? It is the effort—with as much creativity and sacrifice as necessary—to give others everlasting and ever-increasing joy[3]—joy in God. If God is most glorified in us when we are most satisfied in him, as we argued in Chapter 2, then living for the glory of God must mean that we live to gladly make others glad in God. Our gladness and our pursuit of their gladness glorifies God. And since gladness in God is the greatest and most lasting happiness, pursuing it is also love. Since the same joy in God both satisfies man and glorifies God, we never have to choose between the motive to love people or to glorify God.[4] By gladly pursuing the gladness of others in God—even at the cost of our lives—we love *them* and honor *God*. This is the opposite of a wasted life.

WE CANNOT MAKE ANYONE GLAD IN GOD

How then do we make others glad in God? That is what the next chapters are about. But first there are two clarifications I should make. The first clarification is that, of course, we can't *make* anyone glad in God. Joy in God is a fruit of the Holy Spirit (Galatians 5:22). It is called "the joy of the *Holy Spirit*" (1 Thessalonians 1:6). It is the work of God: "May the *God* of hope fill you with all joy and peace" (Romans 15:13). It is the effect of God's grace: "We want you to know, brothers, about the *grace* of God that has been given among the churches of Macedonia, for in a severe test of affliction, their abundance of *joy* and their extreme poverty have overflowed in a wealth of generosity" (2 Corinthians 8:1-2). Joy in God is awakened in the heart when God graciously opens our eyes to see the glory of Christ in the Gospel (2 Corinthians 4:4).

Nevertheless, even though joy in God is ultimately a gift of God, he uses means to bring people into the fullness of it. Paul described his whole ministry as laboring for the joy of others. "Not that we lord it over your faith, but we *work with you for your joy*" (2 Corinthians 1:24). He said to the Philippian church that the reason God would let him live was "for your progress and *joy* in the faith" (Philippians 1:25). Jesus said that his own words were the means God would use to give joy to his disciples: "These things I have spoken to you, that my *joy* may be in you, and that your *joy* may be full" (John 15:11). He also said that prayer was a means of joy: "Until now you have asked nothing in my name. *Ask*, and you will receive, that your *joy* may be full" (John 16:24). The list of means could go on. But the point here is simply to show that there are things we can do to make people glad in God, provided God blesses our efforts with his decisive grace.

MAKING OTHERS GLAD IN GOD IS A MASSIVE THING

The second clarification is that gladness in God is not a peripheral religious experience. When I speak of making people glad in God, I have in mind all the saving work that God has done from beginning to end. I am not saying that gladness is the whole of salvation. I am saying that gladness in God is the goal of all saving work, and the experiential essence of what it means to be saved. Without this joy in God, there would be no salvation.

So when I speak of making someone glad in God, I include the *plan and grace of God* "which he gave us in Christ Jesus before the ages began" (2 Timothy 1:9). I include the all-sufficient *redeeming work of Christ* in death and resurrection (Romans 3:24-26). I include the divine work of *new birth* that gives us a new nature (John 3:3-7; 1 Peter 1:3, 23). I include the God-given change of mind called *repentance* that turns away from sin and turns to God for help (2 Timothy 2:25; Acts 3:19; 26:20). I include *faith* in Jesus Christ that embraces him as the Savior and Lord and supreme Treasure of life (Philippians 3:7-9). I include the progressive change into Christlikeness called *sanctification* (Romans 6:22; 8:29). I include the entire *life of love* that counts it more blessed to give than to receive (Acts 20:35). And I include the *total renewal* of body, mind, heart, relationships, and society that happens partially in this age, by the inbreaking of God's kingdom, and then completely at the consummation of God's purposes in the age to come (Acts 3:21; Romans 8:23).

When I speak of gladness in God, therefore, I mean a gladness that has roots in God's eternal decree, was purchased by the blood of Christ, springs up in the newborn heart because of God's Spirit, awakens in repentance and faith, constitutes the essence of sanctification and Christlikeness, and gives rise to a life of love and a passion for redeeming the world after the image of God. Gladness in God is a massive reality planned and purchased and produced by God in the lives of his elect for the glory of his name.

WHAT THEN SHOULD WE DO?

With those two clarifications, I ask again, what should we do to make people glad in God? What paths of risk and sacrifice should we take in our passion for the supremacy of God in all things, and in our zeal to magnify Christ, and in our single-minded commitment to boast only in the cross? That is what the next chapters are about.

NOTES

1   For more, see John Piper, *God Is the Gospel: Meditation on God's Love as the Gift of Himself* (Wheaton, Ill.: Crossway Books, 2005).

2   Robert Murray M'Cheyne, *Sermons of M'Cheyne* (Edinburgh: n. p., 1848), 482. Italics added. Quoted in Timothy J. Keller, *Ministries of Mercy: The Call of the Jericho Road* (Phillipsburg, N.J.: Presbyterian & Reformed, 1997), 40.

3   I say "ever-increasing" not because we move from sadness to gladness over time in heaven, but because we go on from one fullness to another. I say this because a finite mind—and we will always be finite—cannot receive the whole of God. He is infinite. Therefore he communicates his infinite fullness to us in degrees forever. There will always be more for a finite mind to see of an infinite God. As we see this, we will be more and more happy. You can see more thoughts on this by Jonathan Edwards in John Piper, *God's Passion for his Glory: Living the Vision of Jonathan Edwards* (Wheaton, Ill.: Crossway Books, 1998), 37.

4   For a more extended treatment of the unity of these two motives in the Christian life, see the chapter, "A Passion for God's Supremacy and Compassion for Man's Soul: Jonathan Edwards on the Unity of Motives for World Missions," in John Piper, *Let the Nations Be Glad: The Supremacy of God in Missions*, 2nd edition (Grand Rapids, Mich.: Baker, 2003), 203-214.

To make others glad in God with an everlasting gladness, our lives must show that he is more precious than life. "Because your steadfast love is better than life, my lips will praise you" (Psalm 63:3). To do this we must make sacrificial life choices rooted in the assurance that magnifying Christ through generosity and mercy is more satisfying than selfishness. If we walk away from risk to keep ourselves safe and solvent, we will waste our lives. This chapter is about the kind of lifestyle that may keep that from happening.

HOW NOT TO BETRAY JESUS

If Christ is an all-satisfying treasure and promises to provide all our needs, even through famine and nakedness, then to live as though we had all the same values as the world would betray him. I have in mind mainly how we use our money and how we feel about our possessions. I hear the haunting words of Jesus, "Do not be anxious, saying, 'What shall we eat?' or 'What shall we drink?' or 'What shall we wear?' For the Gentiles seek after all these things" (Matthew 6:31-32). In other words, if we look like our lives are devoted to getting and maintaining things, we will look like the world, and that will not make Christ look great. He will look like a religious side-interest that may be useful for escaping hell in the end, but doesn't make much difference in what we live and love here. He will not look like an all-satisfying treasure. And that will not make others glad in God.

If we are exiles and refugees on earth (1 Peter 2:11), and if our citizenship is in heaven (Philippians 3:20), and if nothing can separate us from the love of Christ (Romans 8:35), and if his steadfast love is better than life (Psalm 63:3), and if all hardship is working for us an eternal weight of glory (2 Corinthians 4:17), then we will give to the winds our fears and "seek first the kingdom of God and his righteousness" (Matthew 6:33). We will count everything as rubbish in comparison with Christ (Philippians 3:7-8). We will "joyfully accept the plundering of our property" for the sake of unpopular acts of mercy (Hebrews 10:34). We will choose " rather to be mistreated with the people of God than to enjoy the fleeting pleasures of sin," and we will count "the reproach of Christ greater wealth than the treasures of Egypt" (Hebrews 11:25-26).

WHY DON'T PEOPLE ASK US ABOUT OUR HOPE?

There is no doubt that if we lived more like this, the world would be more likely to consider whether Jesus is an all-satisfying Treasure. He would look like one. When was the last time someone asked you about "the reason for the hope that is in you"? That's what Peter said we should always be ready to give an answer for: "Always be prepared to make a defense to anyone who asks you for a reason for the hope that is in you" (1 Peter 3:15).

Why don't people ask us about our hope? The answer is probably that we look as if we hope in the same things they do. Our lives don't look like they are on the Calvary road, stripped down for sacrificial love, serving others with the sweet assurance that we don't need to be rewarded in this life. Our reward is great in heaven (Matthew 5:12)! "You will be repaid at the resurrection of the just" (Luke 14:14). If we believed this more deeply, others might see the worth of God and find in him their gladness.

THE CREDIBILITY OF CHRIST HANGS ON HOW WE USE OUR MONEY

The issue of money and lifestyle is not a side issue in the Bible. The credibility of Christ in the world hangs on it. "Fifteen percent of everything Christ said relates to this topic—more than his teachings on heaven and hell combined."[1] Listen to this refrain that runs all through his teachings:

- "You lack one thing: go, sell all you have and give to the poor, and you will have treasure in heaven; and come, follow me" (Mark 10:21).
- "Blessed are you who are poor, for yours is the kingdom of God. . . . But woe to you who are rich, for you have received your consolation" (Luke 6:20, 24).
- "Any of you who does not renounce all that he has cannot be my disciple" (Luke 14:33).
- "It is easier for a camel to go through the eye of a needle than for a rich person to enter the kingdom of God" (Luke 18:25).
- "One's life does not consist in the abundance of his possessions" (Luke 12:15).
- "Seek first the kingdom of God and his righteousness, and all these things will be added to you" (Matthew 6:33).

- "Sell your possessions and give to the needy. Provide yourselves with moneybags . . . in the heavens" (Luke 12:33).
- "Zacchaeus . . . said to the Lord, 'Behold, Lord, the half of my goods I give to the poor. . . .' And Jesus said to him, 'Today salvation has come to this house'" (Luke 19:8-9).
- "The kingdom of heaven is like treasure hidden in a field, which a man found and covered up. Then in his joy he goes and sells all that he has and buys that field" (Matthew 13:44).
- "[Jesus] saw a poor widow put in two small copper coins. And he said, 'Truly, I tell you, this poor widow has put in more than all of them'" (Luke 21:2-3).
- "But God said to him, 'Fool! This night your soul is required of you, and the things you have prepared, whose will they be?' So is the one who lays up treasure for himself and is not rich toward God" (Luke 12:20-21).
- "Foxes have holes, and birds of the air have nests, but the Son of Man has nowhere to lay his head. . . . Follow me" (Luke 9:58-59).

HAZARDOUS LIBERALITY

Over and over Jesus is relentless in his radical call to a wartime lifestyle and a hazardous liberality. I say "hazardous" because of that story about the widow. She gave her last penny to the temple ministry. Most of us would call her foolish or, more delicately, imprudent. But there is not a word of criticism from Jesus:

> And a poor widow came and put in two small copper coins, which make a penny. And he called his disciples to him and said to them, "Truly, I say to you, this poor widow has put in more than all those who are contributing to the offering box. For they all contributed out of their abundance, but she

out of her poverty has put in everything she had, all she had to live on." *(Mark 12:42-44, emphasis added)*

The point here is not that everyone should give everything away. The point is: Jesus loves faith-filled risk for the glory of God. I don't have laws to give you concerning the particulars of how to spend your money, any more than Jesus did. I simply want to point to Jesus and let his word have its shocking and saving effect on us.

USE MONEY TO SHOW THAT GOD, NOT POSSESSIONS, IS OUR TREASURE

Jesus' emphasis on money and possessions is picked up throughout the New Testament. There are the stories in the book of Acts ("They were selling their possessions . . . and distributing the proceeds . . . as any had need," Acts 2:45). There are the words of the apostle Paul ("In a severe test of affliction, their abundance of joy and their extreme poverty have overflowed in a wealth of generosity. . . . God loves a cheerful giver," 2 Corinthians 8:2; 9:7). There are the words of James, the brother of Jesus ("Its flower falls, and its beauty perishes. So also will the rich man fade away in the midst of his pursuits," James 1:11).

The issue is pervasive because it is crucial for the witness of the church. If we want to make people glad in God, our lives must look as if God, not possessions, is our joy. Our lives must look as if we use our possessions to make people glad in God—especially the most needy.

WHY I USE THE PHRASE "WARTIME LIFESTYLE"

Sometimes I use the phrase "wartime lifestyle" or "wartime mind-set." The phrase is helpful—but also lopsided. For me it is mainly helpful. It tells me that there is a war going on in the world between Christ and Satan, truth and falsehood, belief and unbelief. It tells me that there are weapons to be funded and used, but that these weapons are not swords or guns or bombs but the Gospel and prayer and self-sacrificing love (2 Corinthians 10:3-5). And it tells me that the stakes of this conflict are higher than any other war in history; they are eternal and infinite: heaven or hell, eternal joy or eternal torment (Matthew 25:46).

I need to hear this message again and again, because I drift into a peacetime mind-set as certainly as rain falls down and flames go up. I am wired by nature to love the same toys that the world loves. I start to fit in. I start to love what others love. I start to call earth "home." Before you know it, I am calling luxuries "needs" and using my money just the way unbelievers do. I begin to forget the war. I don't think much about people perishing. Missions and unreached peoples drop out of my mind. I stop dreaming about the triumphs of grace. I sink into a secular mind-set that looks first to what man can do, not what God can do. It is a terrible sickness. And I thank God for those who have forced me again and again toward a wartime mind-set.

WHAT IT LOOKS LIKE IN WARTIME

I thank God for Ralph Winter, for example, who not only wrote powerfully about a wartime lifestyle, but has lived it as a missionary, professor, founder of the U. S. Center for World Mission, and tireless advocate for the unreached peoples of the world. He gave the following vivid illustration of the difference between a wartime and a peacetime mentality about the use of our possessions.

> The Queen Mary, lying in repose in the harbor at Long Beach, California, is a fascinating museum of the past. Used both as a luxury liner in peacetime and a troop transport during the Second World War, its present status as a museum the length of three football fields affords a stunning contrast

between the lifestyles appropriate in peace and war. On one side of a partition you see the dining room reconstructed to depict the peacetime table setting that was appropriate to the wealthy patrons of high culture for whom a dazzling array of knives and forks and spoons held no mysteries. On the other side of the partition the evidences of wartime austerities are in sharp contrast. One metal tray with indentations replaces fifteen plates and saucers. Bunks, not just double but eight tiers high, explain why the peace-time complement of 3000 gave way to 15,000 people on board in wartime. How repugnant to the peacetime masters this transformation must have been! To do it took a national emergency, of course. The survival of a nation depended on it. The essence of the Great Commission today is that the survival of many millions of people depends on its fulfillment.[2]

Given the vulnerability of my heart to the seduction of the peacetime mind-set, which is pushed into my mind every day by media and entertainment, I need these images and these reminders. We are at war, whether the stocks are falling or climbing, whether the terrorists are hitting or hiding, whether we are healthy or sick. Both pleasure and pain are laced with poison, ready to kill us with the diseases of pride or despair. The repeated biblical warning to "be alert"[3] fits the wartime image. And I need this warning every day.

WHY NOT SPEAK OF A "SIMPLE LIFESTYLE"?

It is more helpful to think of a wartime lifestyle than a merely simple lifestyle. Simplicity may have a romantic ring and a certain aesthetic appeal that is foreign to the dirty business of mercy in the dangerous places of the world. Simplicity may also overlook the fact that, in wartime, major expenses for complex weapons and troop training are needed. These may not look simple, and may be very expensive, but the whole country sacrifices to make them happen. Simplicity may be inwardly directed and may benefit no one else. A wartime lifestyle implies that there is a great and worthy cause for which to spend and be spent (2 Corinthians 12:15).

WASTING LIFE MEANS LOSING OUR LIVES BY TRYING TO SAVE THEM

"Being spent" may sound dour. It is not. It is life-giving when we are spent to make others glad in God. Jesus taught us that "whoever would save his life will lose it, but whoever loses his life for my sake and the gospel's will save it" (Mark 8:35). This has application to individuals on their way to heaven, and to cultures on their way to extinction. Again Ralph Winter illustrates:

> America today is a "save yourself" society if there ever was one. But does it really work? The underdeveloped societies suffer from one set of diseases: tuberculosis, malnutrition, pneumonia, parasites, typhoid, cholera, typhus, etc. Affluent America has virtually invented a whole new set of diseases: obesity, arteriosclerosis, heart disease, strokes, lung cancer, venereal disease, cirrhosis of the liver, drug addiction, alcoholism, divorce, battered children, suicide, murder. Take your choice. Labor-saving machines have turned out to be body-killing devices. Our affluence has allowed both mobility and isolation of the nuclear family, and as a result, our divorce courts, our prisons and our mental institutions are flooded. In saving ourselves we have nearly lost ourselves.[4]

Using our possessions in a way that makes the most needy glad in God would save us in more ways than one. It would confirm that Christ is our Treasure, and thus keep us on the path to heaven. And it would transform our society, which is driven by the suicidal craving to satisfy itself with no joy in Christ and no love for the needy. To rescue us from this tragedy we should ponder seriously the importance of a wartime lifestyle.

WARTIME AT THE MICROBIOLOGICAL LEVEL

In recent years Ralph Winter has waved another wartime flag. It's worth waving here. God may use it to send some of you in a direction of ministry you never thought was ministry. Winter has been calling our attention to the effects of sin and Satan at the microbiological level where some of the most horrific devastation of God's good creation happens.

> Satan has, horrifyingly, employed his rebellious freedom in the development of destructive germs and viruses at the microbial level, which today account for one third of all deaths on the planet. What the Bible calls simply "pestilence," is a scourge to animals and humans alike. Yet our popular theology does not clearly recognize this as a work of Satan which God expects us to combat as part of His mission.
>
> But, if missionaries do not preach about a God who is interested in all suffering, all distortions of His creative handiwork, on all these levels we are simply misrepresenting the full scope of His pervasive love and concern—His very nature. . . .
>
> In Vietnam ten Americans died every day on the average during the entire ten years of that war. And, our government poured uncalculated billions into that conflict to extricate our people from it.
>
> However, right now not ten but 1,500 Americans die every day of cancer. Yet our government truly puts only pennies in that direction: 80% of it diverted to HIV/AIDS research, the 20% that ends up in cancer research going almost entirely to evaluating treatments not working toward prevention. I understand that all 40 funded projects of the

federal National Cancer Institute are focused on chemo and radiation treatment, not prevention.

It's like getting caught up in 150 Vietnam wars at the same time—as far as battle deaths are concerned. And yet we act as though no war exists! How can the consciousness of America be aroused to the fact that one third of all women and half of all men will contract cancer before they die?[5]

It fully accords with the intention of this book that thousands of Christians would hear this challenge from Dr. Winter and give their lives in science and research, as well as medical missions, to wage war against disease and suffering, and thus display the beauty and power of Christ. What kinds of sacrifices should we make for such combat with the enemy?

WHEN A BOBBY PIN MATTERED

We have seen the sacrifices that military people made in wartime during World War II. But it wasn't just the military that changed its priorities. The whole country did, just like the whole church could today. During World War II,

the entire nation . . . seemed overnight to have snapped out of its Depression-era lethargy. Everyone scrambled to be of help. Rubber was needed for the war effort, and gasoline, and metal. A women's basketball game at Northwestern University was stopped so that the referee and all ten players could scour the floor for a lost bobby pin. Americans pitched in to support strict rationing programs and their boys turned out as volunteers in various collection "drives." Soon butter and milk were restricted along with canned goods and meat. Shoes became scarce, and paper, and silk. People grew "victory gardens" and drove at the gas-saving "victory speed" of thirty-five miles an hour. "Use it up, wear it out, make it do, or do without?" became a popular slogan. Air-raid sirens and blackouts were scrupulously obeyed. America sacrificed.[6]

Such images are for me very powerful. Secondarily, they make me appreciate the benefits of freedom and prosperity. But primarily they rebuke me for my frivolous living and inspire me to make my life count for something more than comfort and worldly success—something God-exalting and eternal.

YES, YES, TO TALK OF WAR IS LOPSIDED

But I admit, as I said above, that the term "wartime lifestyle" or "wartime mind-set" is lopsided. After one sermon in which I used these terms one person wrote to me and asked, "When you stress the imagery of wartime living, do you leave any room for aspects of life that are not part of war, like art or leisure? Are there not other images of the Christian life that are more restful than war?"

Here is the answer I gave in my next message:

The answer is, yes, absolutely, there are other images of the Christian life that are more restful. "The LORD is my Shepherd; I shall not want. He makes me lie down in green pastures. He leads me beside still waters" (Psalm 23:1-2). That is a very different image than bombs dropping and blood flowing. "Come to me, all who labor and are heavy laden, and I will give you rest" (Matthew 11:28). "Even to your old age I am he, and to gray hairs I will carry you. I have made, and I will bear; I will carry and will save" (Isaiah 46:4).

And yes, there is a proper time and place for the Christian to benefit from, evaluate, and transform the whole range of human culture. In fact, it is virtually impossible not to be a part of our modern, Western culture; and if we do *not* think in terms of measured appropriation, biblical evaluation, and thoughtful transformation, we will probably be consumed by the culture, and won't even know that we are more American than we are Christian.

So, yes, by all means, use *all* the images of Scripture (not just war) to shape your life. And then let your radically Christian, God-enthralled, Christ-treasuring, giving-oriented life engage and shape your culture.

But my sense is that in the prosperous West, the danger in the church is not that there are too many overly zealous people who care too deeply about the lost, and invest hazardously in the cause of the Gospel, and ruin their lives with excessive mercy to the poor. For every careless saint who burns himself out and breaks up his family with misdirected zeal, I venture, there are a thousand who coast with the world, treating Jesus like a helpful add-on, but not as an all-satisfying, all-authoritative King in the cause of love.

THE RUINOUS ETHIC OF MERE AVOIDANCE

One of the marks of this peacetime mind-set is what I call an avoidance ethic. In wartime we ask different questions about what to do with our lives than we do in peacetime. We ask: What can I do to advance the cause? What can I do to bring the victory? What sacrifice can I make or what risk can I take to insure the joy of triumph? In peacetime we tend to ask, What can I do to be more comfortable? To have more fun? To avoid trouble and, possibly, avoid sin?

If we are going to pay the price and take the risks it will cost to make people glad in God, we move beyond the avoidance ethic. This way of life is utterly inadequate to waken people to the beauty of Christ. Avoiding fearful trouble and forbidden behaviors impresses almost no one. The avoidance ethic by itself is not Christ-commending or God-glorifying. There are many disciplined unbelievers who avoid the same behaviors Christians do. Jesus calls us to something far more radical than that.

THE WRONG QUESTIONS AND THE RIGHT ONES

People who are content with the avoidance ethic generally ask the wrong question about behavior. They ask, What's wrong with it? What's wrong with this movie? Or this music? Or this game? Or these companions? Or this way of relaxing? Or this investment? Or this restaurant? Or shopping at this store? What's wrong with going to the cabin every weekend? Or having a cabin? This kind of question will rarely yield a lifestyle that commends Christ as all-satisfying and makes people glad in God. It simply results in a list of don'ts. It feeds the avoidance ethic.

The better questions to ask about possible behaviors is: How will this help me treasure Christ more? How will it help me show that I do treasure Christ? How will it help me know Christ or display Christ? The Bible says, "Whether you eat or drink, or whatever you do, do all to the glory of God" (1 Corinthians 10:31). So the question is mainly positive, not negative. How can I portray God as glorious in this action? How can I enjoy making much of him in this behavior?

CLEAN NOSES AND QUALITY FAMILY TIME IS NOT LIFE

Oh, how many lives are wasted by people who believe that the Christian life means simply avoiding badness and providing for the family. So there is no adultery, no stealing, no killing, no embezzlement, no fraud—just lots of hard work during the day, and lots of TV and PG-13 videos in the evening (during quality family time), and lots of fun stuff on the weekend—woven around church (mostly). This is life for millions of people. Wasted life. We were created for more, far more.

There is an old saying: "No man ever lamented on his dying bed, 'I wish I had spent more time at the office.'" The point being made is usually that when you are about to die, money suddenly looks like what it really is, useless for lasting happiness, while relationships become precious. It's true. When my mother was killed in 1974, I wrote to the chairman of my department at Bethel College, where I was teaching, and reversed my request to teach an overload the next semester to make more money. Standing beside your mother's grave with a wife and child makes things look different. Money loses its pull.

But that saying about spending less time at the office can be misleading. We need to add this: No one will ever want to say to the Lord of the universe five minutes after death, I spent every night playing games and watching clean TV with my family because I loved them so much. I think the Lord will say, "That did not make me look like a treasure in your town. You should have done something besides provide for yourself and your family. And TV, as you should have known, was not a good way to nurture your family or your own soul."

TELEVISION, THE GREAT LIFE-WASTER

Television is one of the greatest life-wasters of the modern age. And, of course, the Internet is running to catch up, and may have caught up. You can be more selective on the Internet, but you can also select worse things with only the Judge of the universe watching. TV still reigns as the great life-waster. The main problem with TV is not how much smut is available, though that is a problem. Just the ads are enough to sow fertile seeds of greed and lust, no matter what program you're watching. The greater problem is banality. A mind fed daily on TV diminishes. Your mind was made to know and love God. Its facility for this great calling is ruined by excessive TV. The content is so trivial and so shallow that the capacity of the mind to think worthy thoughts withers, and the capacity of the heart to feel deep emotions shrivels. Neil Postman shows why.

> What is happening in America is that television is transforming all serious public business into junk. . . . Television disdains exposition, which is serious, sequential, rational, and complex. It offers instead a mode of discourse in which everything is accessible, simplistic, concrete, and above all, entertaining. As a result, America is the world's first culture in jeopardy of amusing itself to death.[7]

THE WEIGHTLESSNESS OF GOD

Since we all live in a world created by television, it is almost impossible to see what has happened to us. The only hope is to read what people were like in previous centuries. Biographies are a great antidote to cultural myopia and chronological snobbery. We have become almost incapable of handling any great truth reverently and deeply. Magnificent things, especially the glory of God, as David Wells says, rest with a kind of "weightlessness" even on the church.

> It is one of the defining marks of Our Time that God is now weightless. I do not mean by this that he is ethereal but rather that he has become unimportant. He rests upon the world so inconsequentially as not to be noticeable. He has lost his saliency for human life. Those who assure the pollsters of their belief in God's existence may nonetheless consider him less interesting than television, his commands less authoritative than their appetites for affluence and influence, his judgment no more awe-inspiring than the evening news, and his truth less compelling than the advertisers' sweet fog of flattery and lies. That is weightlessness. It is a

condition we have assigned him after having nudged him out to the periphery of our secularized life. . . . Weightlessness tells us nothing about God but everything about ourselves, about our condition, about our psychological disposition to exclude God from our reality.[8]

SORTING OUT SUDAN AND PANTY HOSE

We have lost our ability to see and savor the complexities of truth and the depths of simplicity. Douglas Groothuis explains the connection between this weakness and television.

> The triumph of the televised image over the word contributes to the depthlessness of postmodern sensibilities. . . . One cannot muse over a television program the way one ponders a character in William Shakespeare or C. S. Lewis, or a Blaise Pascal parable, or a line from a T. S. Eliot poem, such as 'But our lot crawls between dry ribs / to keep its metaphysics warm.' No one on television could utter such a line seriously. It would be "bad television"—too abstract, too poetic, too deep, just not entertaining. . . . [Not only that] but the images appear and disappear and reappear without a proper rational context. An attempt at a sobering news story about slavery in the Sudan is followed by a lively advertisement for Disneyland, followed by an appeal to purchase panty hose that will make any woman irresistible, etc., ad nauseum.[9]

Therefore the man who stands before God with his well-kept avoidance ethic and his protest that he did not spend too much time at the office but came home and watched TV with his family will probably not escape the indictment that he wasted his life. Jesus rebuked his disciples with words that easily apply to this man: "Even sinners work hard, avoid gross sin, watch TV at night, and do fun stuff on the weekend. What more are you doing than the others?" (see Luke 6:32-34; Matthew 5:47).

INSPIRING SACRIFICE FOR LESSER CAUSES

In fact, in wartime sinners often rise to remarkable levels of sacrifice for causes that cannot compare with Christ. The greatest cause in the world is joyfully rescuing people from hell, meeting their earthly needs, making them glad in God, and doing it with a kind, serious pleasure that makes Christ look like the Treasure he is. No war on earth was ever fought for a greater cause or a greater king.

But oh, what bold risks and daring sacrifices these lesser causes have inspired! On February 19, 1945, the battle for Iwo Jima began. It was a barren, eight-mile-square island six hundred miles south of Tokyo, guarded by 22,000 Japanese prepared to fight to the death (which they did). They were protecting two air strips that America needed in the strategic effort to contain Japanese aggression after Pearl Harbor and preserve the liberty that America cherished. It was a high cause, and the courageous sacrifice was stunning.

The hard statistics show the sacrifice made by Colonel Johnson's 2nd Battalion: 1,400 boys [many still teenagers] landed on D-Day; 288 replacements were provided as the battle went on, a total of 1,688. Of these, 1,511 had been killed or wounded. Only 177 walked off the island. And of the final 177, 91 had been wounded at least once and returned to battle.

It had taken twenty-two crowded transports to bring the 5th Division to the island. The survivors fit comfortably onto eight departing ships.

The American boys had killed about 21,000 Japanese, but suffered more than 26,000 casualties doing so. This would be the only battle in the Pacific where the invaders suffered higher casualties than the defenders.

The Marines fought in World War II for forty-three months. Yet in one month on Iwo Jima, one third of their total deaths occurred. They left behind the Pacific's largest cemeteries: nearly 6,800 graves in all; mounds with their crosses and stars. Thousands of families would not have the solace of a body to bid farewell: just the abstract information that the Marine had "died in the performance of his duty" and was buried in a plot, aligned in a row with numbers on his grave. Mike lay in Plot 3, Row 5, Grave 694; Harlon in Plot 4, Row 6, Grave 912; Franklin in Plot 8, Row 7, Grave 2189.

When I think of Mike, Harlon, and Franklin there, I think of the message someone had chiseled outside the cemetery:

When you go home
Tell them for us and say
For your tomorrow
We gave our today[10]

O LORD, DON'T LET ME WASTE MY LIFE!

I am deeply moved by the courage and carnage on Iwo Jima. As I read the pages of this history, everything in me cries out, "O Lord, don't let me waste my life!" Let me come to the end—whether soon or late—and be able to say to a family, a church, a city, and the unreached peoples of the earth, "For your tomorrow, I gave my today. Not just for your tomorrow on earth, but for the countless tomorrows of your ever-increasing gladness in God." The closer I looked at the individual soldiers in this World War II history, the more I felt a passion that my life would count, and that I would be able to die well.

As rainy morning wore into afternoon and the fighting bogged down, the Marines continued to take casualties. Often it was the corpsmen [medics] themselves who died as they tried to preserve life. William Hoopes of Chattanooga was crouching beside a medic named Kelly, who put his head above a protective ridge and placed binoculars to his eyes—just for an instant—to spot a sniper who was peppering his area. In that instant the sniper shot him through the Adam's apple. Hoopes, a pharmacist's mate himself, struggled frantically to save his friend. "I took my forceps and reached into his neck to grasp the artery and pinch it off," Hoopes recalled. "His blood was spurting. He had no speech but his eyes were on me. He knew I was trying to save his life. I tried everything in the world. I couldn't do it. I tried. The blood was so slippery. I couldn't get the artery. I was trying so hard. And all the while he just looked at me. He looked directly into my face. The last thing he did as the blood spurts became less and less was to pat me on the arm as if to say, 'That's all right.' Then he died."[11]

In this heart-breaking moment I want to be Hoopes and I want to be Kelly. I want to be able to say to suffering and perishing people, "I tried everything in the world. . . . I was trying so hard." And I want to be able to say to those around me when I die, "It's all right. To live is Christ, and to die is gain."

WHEN THE TRIFLING FOG CLEARS

At these moments, when the trifling fog of life clears and I see what I am really on earth to do, I groan over the petty pursuits that waste so many lives—and so much of mine. Just think of the magnitude of sports—a whole section of the daily newspaper. But there is no section on God. Think of the endless resources for making your home and garden more comfortable and impressive. Think of how many tens of thousands of dollars you can spend to buy more car than you need. Think of the time and energy and conversation that go into entertainment and leisure and what we call "fun stuff." And add to that now the computer that artificially recreates the very games that are already so distant from reality; it is like a multi-layered dreamworld of insignificance expanding into nothingness.

CONSUMED WITH CLOTHES

Or think about clothes. What a tragedy to see so many young people obsessed with what they wear and how they look. Even Christian youth seem powerless to ask greater questions than "What's wrong with it?" Like: Will these clothes help me magnify Christ? Will they point people to him as the manifest Treasure of my life? Will they highlight my personhood, created in the image of God to serve, or will they highlight my sexuality? Or my laziness? Trust me, I'm not hung up on clothes. There are some pretty radical, Christ-exalting reasons to dress down. My plea is that you be more like a dolphin and less like a jellyfish in the sea of fashion—and of contra-fashion (which is just as tyrannizing).

Go beyond one teenager who wrote to the Minneapolis *Star Tribune* in response to a letter to the editor:

> As a teenager, what you wear is unfortunately becoming more important. Honestly even I find some of the clothes that I wear offensive. The letter spoke of girls being able to dress fashionably and sensibly. Show me how that's possible, and I'll do it.
>
> Most of my friends often are not comfortable with what is popular, but we wear it anyway. Standing out is just not always worth the struggle. Society tells us to be different, yet mainstream.
>
> How do you dress to please yourself, your parents and your peers? You can't. Teens end up compromising their values to fit in. If we intend to make it through high school, or even junior high, without being tormented then we must dress to please our peers.

We are the up-and-coming leaders of this nation, and we must see what we have become and change.[12]

WHERE ARE THE YOUNG RADICALS FOR CHRIST?

When I stand, as it were, on the shores of Iwo Jima and let myself reenact those hours of courage and sacrifice, and remember that they were young, I cannot make peace with the petty preoccupations of most American life. One of them was really young. I read his story and wanted to speak to every youth group in America and say, Do you want to see what *cool* is? Do you want to see something a thousand times more impressive than a triple double? Well, listen up about Jacklyn Lucas.

> He'd fast-talked his way into the Marines at fourteen, fooling the recruits with his muscled physique. . . . Assigned to drive a truck in Hawaii, he had grown frustrated; he wanted to fight. He stowed away on a transport out of Honolulu, surviving on food passed along to him by sympathetic leathernecks on board.
>
> He landed on D-Day [at Iwo Jima] without a rifle. He grabbed one lying on the beach and fought his way inland.
>
> Now, on D+1, Jack and three comrades were crawling through a trench when eight Japanese sprang in front of them. Jack shot one of them through the head. Then his rifle jammed. As he struggled with it a grenade landed at his feet. He yelled a warning to the others and rammed the grenade into the soft ash. Immediately, another rolled in. Jack Lucas, seventeen, fell on both grenades. "Luke, you're gonna die," he remembered thinking. . . .
>
> Aboard the hospital ship Samaritan the doctors could scarcely believe it. "Maybe he was too damned young and too damned tough to die," one said. He endured twenty-one reconstructive operations and became the nation's youngest

Medal of Honor winner—and the only high school freshman to receive it.[13]

As I read that, I thought of all the things that high school kids think is cool. I sat on the porch where I was reading and thought, *O God, who will get in their face and give them something to live for? They waste their days in a trance of insignificance, trying to look cool or talk cool or walk cool. They don't have a clue what cool is.*

One more story to clarify what is cool. It's about Ray Dollins, a fighter pilot at Iwo Jima.

> The first wave of amtracs headed for shore. The Marine fighter planes were finishing up their low strafing runs. And as the last pilot began to pull his Corsair aloft, Japanese sprang to their guns and riddled the plane with flak. The pilot, Major Ray Dollins, tried to gain altitude as he headed out over the ocean so as to avoid a deadly crash into the Marines headed for the beach, but his plane was too badly damaged. Lieutenant Keith Wells watched it from the amtrac. . . . "We could see him in the cockpit," Wells said, "and he was trying everything. He was heading straight down for a group of approaching 'tracs filled with Marines. At the last second he flipped the plane over on its back and aimed it into the water between two waves of tanks. We watched the water exploding into the air."
>
> Military personnel listening to the flight radio network from the ships could not only see Dollins go down; they could hear his last words into his microphone. They were a defiant parody.

> *Oh, what a beautiful morning,*
> *Oh, what a beautiful day,*
> *I've got a terrible feeling*
> *Everything's coming my way.*[14]

Of course, we do not use the word *cool* to describe true greatness. It is a small word. That's the point. It's cheap. And it's what millions of young people live for. Who confronts them with urgency and tears? Who pleads with them not to waste their lives? Who takes them by the collar, so to speak, and loves them enough to show them a life so radical and so real and so costly and Christ-saturated that they feel the emptiness and triviality of their CD collection and their pointless conversations about passing celebrities? Who will waken what lies latent in their souls, untapped—a longing not to waste their lives?

MY HEART'S PLEA

Oh, that young and old would turn off the television, take a long walk, and dream about feats of courage for a cause ten thousand times more important than American democracy—as precious as that is. If we would dream and if we would pray, would not God answer? Would he withhold from us a life of joyful love and mercy and sacrifice that magnifies Christ and makes people glad in God? I plead with you, as I pray for myself, set your face like flint to join Jesus on the Calvary road. "Let us go to him outside the camp and bear the reproach he endured. For here we have no lasting city, but we seek the city that is to come" (Hebrews 13:13-14). When they see our sacrificial love—radiant with joy—will they not say, "Christ is great"?

NOTES

1   Randy Alcorn, *The Treasure Principle* (Sisters, Ore.: Multnomah, 2001), 8.

2   Ralph Winter, "Reconsecration to a Wartime, not a Peacetime, Lifestyle," in *Perspectives on the World Christian Movement: A Reader*, 2nd edition, eds. Ralph D. Winter and Steven C. Hawthorne (Pasadena, Ca.: William Carey Library, 1999), 705.

3   Matthew 24:42; 25:13; 26:41; Acts 20:31; 1 Corinthians 16:13; Ephesians 6:18; Colossians 4:2; 1 Thessalonians 5:6; 1 Peter 5:8.

4 Ralph Winter, "Reconsecration to a Wartime, not a Peacetime, Lifestyle," 706.

5 Cited from http://www.verbo.org/site/winter.htm [accessed 4-2-03]. To clarify the relation between Satan's freedom and God's sovereignty, I would stress that Satan is real and that God gives him permission (lengthening his leash, as it were) to exploit the divine curse on creation because of sin (Romans 8:20-23), but that God remains in control of the world in all of its parts. There is no contradiction between saying that God ultimately controls all things and saying that we should labor to triumph over disease, resist injustice, and win people to Christ. Our labor is part of his way of accomplishing his sovereign plan. See John Piper, "God's Pleasure in All That He Does" (Chapter Two), in *The Pleasures of God: Meditations on God's Delight in Being God* (Sisters, Ore.: Multnomah, 2000), 47-76.

6 James Bradley, *Flags of Our Fathers* (New York: Bantam, 2000), 62.

7 Neil Postman, "Amusing Ourselves to Death," *Et Cetera* (Spring 1985): 15, 18. See his book by the same title, *Amusing Ourselves to Death: Public Discourse in the Age of Show Business* (New York: Viking, 1985).

8 David Wells, *God in the Wasteland: The Reality of Truth in a World of Fading Dreams* (Grand Rapids, Mich.: Eerdmans, 1994), 88, 90.

9 Douglas R. Groothuis, "How the Bombarding Images of TV Culture Undermine the Power of Words," *Modern Reformation*, 10 (January/February 2001): 35-36. Available online at http://www.modernreformation.org/mr01/janfeb/mr0101bombardingtv.html.

10 Bradley, *Flags of Our Fathers*, 246-247. This book is the story of the Battle of Iwo Jima woven together with the lives of the six flag raisers in the famous Iwo Jima Memorial, told by the son of John Bradley, one of the soldiers in the Memorial.

11 Ibid., 188.

12 Megan Heggemeir, "For Teenagers, Fashion Is Key to Fitting in," *Minneapolis Star Tribune* (November 16, 2002): A23.

13 Bradley, *Flags of Our Fathers*, 174-175.

14 Ibid., 161-162.

CHAPTER 8
MAKING MUCH OF CHRIST FROM 8 TO 5

It would be a mistake to infer from the call to wartime living in the previous chapter that Christians should quit their jobs and go to "war"—say, to become missionaries or pastors or full-time relief workers. That would be a fundamental misunderstanding of where the war is being fought. Of course, the battles are raging spiritually (without bombs or bayonets) among unreached peoples of the world where the King of kings has sent his selfless "troops" with the gospel of peace and is gathering a happy people for himself. This is the glorious work of frontier missions. I will argue later that it is a magnificent calling; and I pray that thousands of you who read this book will hear it and go to those front lines.

THE WAR IS NOT GEOGRAPHICAL

But make no mistake, the "war" that I have in mind when I speak of a "wartime mind-set" or a "wartime lifestyle" is not being fought along geographical lines. It is being fought first along the line between good and evil in every human heart, especially the hearts of Christians where Christ has staked his claim, and where he means to be totally triumphant. The "war" is being fought along the line between sin and righteousness in every family. It is being fought along the line between truth and false-hood in every school . . . between justice and injustice in every legislature . . . between integrity and corruption in every office . . . between love and hate in every ethnic group . . . between pride and humility in every sport . . . between the beautiful and the ugly in every art . . . between right doctrine and wrong doctrine in every church . . . and between sloth and diligence between coffee breaks. It is not a waste to fight the battle for truth and faith and love on any of these fronts.

The war is not primarily spatial or physical—though its suc-cesses and failures have physical effects. Therefore, the secular vocations of Christians are a war zone. There are spiritual adver-saries to be defeated (that is, evil spirits and sins, not people); and there is beautiful moral high ground to be gained for the glory of God. You don't waste you life by *where* you work, but *how* and *why*.

SECULAR IS NOT BAD, BUT STRATEGIC

Please don't hear in the phrase "secular vocation" any unspiri-tual or inferior comparison to "church vocation" or "mission vocation" or "spiritual vocation." I simply mean the vocations that are not structurally connected to the church. There is such a thing as being *in* the world but not *of* the world, as Jesus taught when he prayed in John 17:15-16, "I do not ask that you take them *out of the world*, but that you keep them from the evil one. *They are not of the world*, just as I am not of the world." So Jesus' intention is that his disciples remain in the world (which is what I mean by "secular jobs"), but that they not be "of the world" (which is why I say we are in a war).

Martin Luther recaptured the biblical teaching of the priesthood of every Christian and blasted the spiritual line between clergy and laity. He agreed that there is a *church* calling and a *secular* calling. But his way of distinguishing them was not based on any superior "spiritual estate."

> It is pure invention that pope, bishops, priests and monks are to be called the "spiritual estate"; princes, lords, artisans and farmers the "temporal estate." That is indeed a fine bit of lying and hypocrisy. . . . All Christians are truly of the "spiritual estate," and there is among them no difference at all but that of office. . . . To make it still clearer. If a little group of pious Christian laymen were taken captive and set down in a wilderness, and had among them no priest consecrated by a bishop, and if there in the wilderness they were to agree in choosing one of themselves, married or unmarried, and were to charge him with the office of baptizing, saying mass, absolving and preaching, such a man would be as truly a priest as though all bishops and popes had consecrated him. . . . There is really no difference between laymen and priests, princes and bishops, "spirituals" and "temporals," as they call them, except that of office and work. . . . A cobbler, a smith, a farmer, each has the work and office of his trade, and yet they are all alike consecrated priests and bishops, and everyone by means of his own work or office must benefit and serve every other, that in this way many kinds of work may be done for the bodily and spiritual welfare of the community, even as all the members of the body serve one another.[1]

The Bible makes it plain that God's will is for his people to be scattered like salt and light among the whole range of secular vocations. Enclaves of Christians living only with Christians and working only with Christians would not accomplish God's whole purpose in the world. That does not mean Christian orders or ministries or mission outposts are wrong. It means they are exceptional. The vast majority of Christians are meant to live in the world and work among unbelievers. This is their "office," their "calling," as Luther would say. We will see why this is God's will in a moment.

PARTNERSHIP OF OX AND PEOPLE

Not everyone should be a missionary or a pastor. There is to be a partnership between goers and senders. Concerning pastors in the church Paul says, "You shall not muzzle an ox when it treads out the grain" (1 Timothy 5:18), meaning: pay your pastor. But that implies that some folks must be earning grain to put under the poor ox's nose. This is also the pattern for missionaries in the New Testament. "Do your best to speed Zenas the lawyer and Apollos on their way; see that they lack nothing" (Titus 3:13). In other words, Not everybody should go to minister with Paul; some should stay behind, work, and supply the ones who go. Similarly Paul planned for the Roman church to be his supply base as he headed for Spain: "I hope to see you in passing as I go to Spain, and to be helped on my journey there by you, once I have enjoyed your company for a while" (Romans 15:24).

He assumed they would be gainfully employed so they could give. That's why he said to the Thessalonian believers, "Work with your hands . . . so that you may . . . be dependent on no one" (1 Thessalonians 4:11-12). In fact, Paul was so provoked by the idle busybodies in Thessalonica that he wrote in a second letter:

> We were not idle when we were with you, nor did we eat anyone's bread without paying for it, but with toil and labor we worked night and day, that we might not be a burden to any of you. . . . If anyone is not willing to work, let him not eat. For we hear that some among you walk in idleness, not busy at work, but busybodies. (2 Thessalonians 3:7-11)

Similarly, he said to the Ephesians, "Let the thief no longer steal, but rather let him labor, doing honest work with his own hands, so that he may have something to share with anyone in need" (Ephesians 4:28).

STAY IN YOUR JOB "WITH GOD"

The call to be a Christian was not a call to leave your secular vocation. That's the clear point of 1 Corinthians 7:17-24. Paul sums up his teaching there with these words: "So, brothers, in whatever condition each was called, there let him remain with God" (verse 24). Paul had a high view of the providence of God—that God had sovereignly "assigned" or "called" unbelievers to positions in life where their conversion would have significant impact for his glory. "Only let each person lead the life that the Lord has *assigned* to him, and to which God has *called* him" (verse 17). Paul does not mean that changing jobs is wrong in the Christian life—otherwise no one could become a vocational pastor or missionary except very young people (unlike Jesus who changed from carpentry to full-time ministry when he was thirty, Luke 3:23). What Paul does mean is that when we are converted we should not jump to the conclusion, my job must change. Rather our thought should be, God has put me here, and I should now display his worth in this job. As verse 24 says, "there let him remain *with God*."

Therefore, the burning question for most Christians should be: How can my life count for the glory of God in my secular vocation? I am assuming from all that has been said in this book so far that the aim of life is the same, whether in a secular vocation or in a church or mission vocation. Our aim is to joyfully magnify Christ—to make him look great by all we do. Boasting only in the cross, our aim is to enjoy making much of him by the way we work. The question is, How? The Bible points to at least six answers.

1. We can make much of God in our secular job through the fellowship that we enjoy with him throughout the day in all our work.

In other words, we enjoy God's being there for us as we listen to his voice, and talk to him, and cast all our burdens on him, and experience his guidance and care. The biblical pointer to this truth is 1 Corinthians 7:24. When you are converted, stay in your job and enjoy God's presence. "In whatever condition each was called, there let him remain *with God.*" These last two words are important. Christians do not just go to work. They go to work "with God." They do not just do a job. They do their job "with God." God is with them.

A More Personal Promise

This is not the same as the general promises made to the church as a whole. God promises to the church corporately, "I will make my dwelling among them and walk among them, and I will be their God, and they shall be my people" (2 Corinthians 6:16). The promise for you in your secular job is different. When the saints are at work in their secular employment, they are scattered. They are not together in church. So the command to "remain there *with God*" is a promise that you may know God's fellowship personally and individually on the job.

Breathing out Continual Thanks to God for All Things

One way to enjoy God's presence and fellowship is through thankful awareness that your ability to do any work at all, including this work, is owing to his grace. "He himself gives to all mankind life and breath and everything" (Acts 17:25). All your faculties of sight and hearing and touch, all your motor skills with hands and legs, all your mental acts of observing and organizing and assessing, all your skills that make you good at this particular job—all these things are God's gifts. To know this can fill you with a sense of continual thankfulness offered up to God in prayer. "I give thanks to you, O Lord my God, with my whole heart, and I will glorify your name forever" (Psalm 86:12). Sometimes the wonder of who God is will rise up in us while we work, and we will whisper his praise: "Bless the LORD, O my soul! O LORD my God, you are very great!" (Psalm 104:1).

When you add to this the awareness that you depend on God for every *future* minute of life and for all the help you need, your thankfulness flows over into faith for each upcoming moment and for the remainder of the day and week and month and year and decade. This is faith in future grace. It can be expressed in prayer to God with biblical words like, "I trust in you, O LORD; I say, 'You are my God'" (Psalm 31:14). Or you can say, "Your steadfast love never ceases; your mercies never come to an end; they are new every morning (and every afternoon!); great is your faithfulness!" (paraphrase of Lamentations 3:22-23).

Taking the Promises to Work

Supporting this thankfulness and praise and trust are the promises of God that you can take to work every day—written in your Bible or memorized in your head. This is the way God speaks to you through the day. He encourages you, "Fear not, for I am with you; be not dismayed, for I am your God; I will strengthen you, I will help you, I will uphold you with my righteous right hand" (Isaiah 41:10). He reminds you that the challenges of the afternoon are not too hard for him to manage: "Behold, I am the LORD, the God of all flesh. Is anything too hard for me?" (Jeremiah 32:27). He tells you not to be anxious, but to ask him for whatever you need (Philippians 4:6), and says, "Cast all your anxieties on me, for I care for you" (paraphrase of 1 Peter 5:7).

And he promises to guide you through the day: "I will instruct you and teach you in the way you should go; I will counsel you with my eye upon you" (Psalm 32:8).

In this way we fellowship with God, listening to him through his Word and thanking him and praising him and calling on him for all we need. It is an honor to God if you stay in your secular job "with God" in this way. This is not a wasted life. God delights in being trusted and enjoyed. It shows his value. And when we remind ourselves that none of these undeserved blessings could be ours apart from the death of Christ in our place, every heartbeat of joy in God becomes a boasting in the cross.

2. We make much of Christ in our secular work by the joyful, trusting, God-exalting design of our creativity and industry.

It is helpful to ask how human beings differ from beavers and hummingbirds and spiders and ants. It helps get at the essence of how humans honor God with their work. These creatures are very hard workers and make very intricate and amazing things. So there must be more to our God-honoring work than such creativity and industry—unless we are willing to say that we glorify God with our work no differently than the animals.

Deputies of God Subduing the Earth for His Glory

What's the difference? Consider the first biblical words about man's creation. "So God created man in his own image, in the image of God he created him; male and female he created them. And God blessed them. And God said to them, 'Be fruitful and multiply and fill the earth and *subdue* it and *have dominion* over the fish of the sea and over the birds of the heavens and over every living thing that moves on the earth'" (Genesis 1:27-28). Our creation in God's image leads directly to our privilege and duty to *subdue* the earth and *have dominion* over it. In other words, we should be busy understanding and shaping and designing and using God's creation in a way that calls attention to his worth and wakens worship.

Being in the image of God means at least that we should image forth God. We should reflect what he is really like. And we should do that not to make ourselves look great (as imagers) but to make him look great (as Creator). People make images of famous people to honor them. God made man in his own image so that he would be seen and enjoyed and honored through what man does.

Then he said, first of all, that what man does is work. He subdues and takes dominion over the earth. This implies that part of what it means to be human is to exercise lordship over creation and give the world shape and order and design that reflects the truth and beauty of God. God makes man, so to speak, his ruling deputy and endows him with God-like rights and capacities to subdue the world—to use it and shape it for good purposes, especially the purpose of magnifying the Creator.

Work Is Not a Curse; Futility Is

So if you go all the way back, before the origin of sin, there are no negative connotations about secular work. According to Genesis 2:2, God himself rested from *his work* of creation, implying that work is a good, God-like thing. And the capstone of that divine work was man, a creature in God's own image designed to carry on the work of ruling and shaping and designing creation. Therefore, at the heart of the meaning of work is *creativity*. If you are God, your work is to create out of nothing. If you are not God, but like God—that is, if you are human— your work is to take what God has made and shape it and use it to make him look great.

How We Differ From Beavers

But here is where the beavers come in. A beaver subdues his surroundings and shapes a dam for a good purpose, a house. He seems to enjoy his work; and even the diligence and skill of the beaver reflects the glory of God's wisdom.

> *All things bright and beautiful,*
> *All creatures great and small,*
> *All things wise and wonderful,*
> *The Lord God made them all.*[2]

And God is glorified in them all. "Let the rivers clap their hands . . . the hills sing for joy . . . and the heavens declare the glory of God" (Psalm 98:8; 19:1). So what is the difference between a human being at work and a beaver at work? Or for that matter, a bee or a hummingbird or an ant? They all work hard; they subdue their surroundings and shape them into amazing structures that serve good purposes. The difference is that humans are morally self-conscious and make choices about their work on the basis of motives that may or may not honor God.

No beaver or bee or hummingbird or ant consciously relies on God. No beaver ponders the divine pattern of order and beauty and makes a moral choice to pursue excellence because God is excellent. No beaver ever pondered the preciousness and purpose of God and decided for God's sake to make a dam for another beaver and not for himself. But humans have all these potentials, because we are created in God's image. We are created to image forth God in these ways. When God commissions us to subdue the earth—to shape it and use it—he doesn't mean do it like a *beaver*. He means do it like a human, a morally self-conscious person who is responsible to do his work intentionally for the glory of his Maker.

To be sure, when God sends us forth to work as his image-bearers, our ditches are to be dug straight, our pipe-fittings are not to leak, our cabinet corners should be flush, our surgical incisions should be clean, our word processing accurate and appealing, and our meals nutritious and attractive, because God is a God of order and beauty and competence. But cats are clean, and ants are industrious, and spiders produce orderly and beautiful works. And all of them are dependent on God. Therefore, the essence of our work as humans must be that it is done in conscious reliance on God's power, and in conscious quest of God's pattern of excellence, and in deliberate aim to reflect God's glory.

Doing Good Work and Sleeping Well

When you work like this—no matter what your vocation is— you can have a sweet sense of peace at the end of the day. It has not been wasted. God has not created us to be idle. Therefore, those who abandon creative productivity lose the joy of God-dependent, world-shaping, God-reflecting purposeful work. "Sweet is the sleep of a laborer, whether he eats little or much, but the full stomach of the rich will not let him sleep" (Ecclesiastes 5:12). Jonathan Edwards made it a rule that personal piety to the neglect of secular duties is hypocritical. He described his own wife ("the person") to illustrate the opposite:

> "Oh how good," said the person once, "it is to work for God in the daytime, and at night to lie down under his smiles!" High experiences and religious affections in this person have not been attended with any disposition at all to neglect the necessary business of a secular calling, to spend time in reading and prayer, and other exercises of devotion; but worldly business has been attended with great alacrity, as part of the service of God; the person declaring that it being done thus, "'tis found to be as good as prayer."[3]

True personal piety feeds the purposeful work of secular vocations rather than undermining it. Idleness does not grow in the soil of fellowship with God. Therefore, people who spend their lives mainly in idleness or frivolous leisure are rarely as happy as those who work. Retired people who are truly happy have sought creative, useful, God-honoring ways to stay active and productive for the sake of man's good and God's glory.

To be sure, we should help each other find and keep work. We should care about the larger problem of unemployment. It is not first an economic problem, though it is that. It is first a theological problem. Human beings are created in the image of God and are endowed with traits of their Creator that fit them for creative, useful, joyful, God-exalting work. Therefore, extensive idleness (when you have the ability to work) brings down the oppression of guilt and futility.

So the second way we make much of God in our secular work is through the joyful, trusting, God-exalting design of our creativity and industry. God created us for work so that by consciously relying on his power and consciously shaping the world after his excellence, we might be satisfied in him, and he might be glorified in us. And when we remember that all this God-exalting creativity and all this joy is only possible for undeserving sinners like us because of the death of Christ, every hour of labor becomes a boasting in the cross.

3. We make much of Christ in our secular work when it confirms and enhances the portrait of Christ's glory that people hear in the spoken Gospel.

There is no point in overstating the case for the value of secular work. It is not the Gospel. By itself, it does not save anyone. In fact, with no spoken words about Jesus Christ, our secular work will not awaken wonder for the glory of Christ. That is why the New Testament modestly calls our work an adornment of the Gospel. In addressing slaves, Paul says they are "to be well-pleasing, not argumentative, not pilfering, but showing all good faith, so that in everything they may *adorn the doctrine of God our Savior*" (Titus 2:9-10). The point here is not to endorse slavery (which Paul undermined more indirectly by calling the converted slave, Onesimus, "no longer . . . a slave but a beloved brother," Philemon 16), but to show that the way we do our work "adorns" the doctrine of God.

In other words, our work is not the beautiful woman, but the necklace. The beautiful woman is the Gospel—"the doctrine of God our Savior." So one crucial meaning of our secular work is that the way we do it will increase or decrease the attractiveness of the Gospel we profess before unbelievers. Of course, the great assumption is that they know we are Christians. The whole point of the text breaks down if there is nothing for our work to "adorn." Thinking that our work will glorify God when people do not know we are Christians is like admiring an effective ad on TV that never mentions the product. People may be impressed but won't know what to buy.

Removing Stumbling Blocks for Faith

There is another place where Paul expresses the modest role of our work in relation to the Gospel. In 1 Thessalonians 4:11 he tells the church, "Aspire to live quietly, and to mind your own affairs, and to work with your hands, as we instructed you, *so that you may live properly before outsiders and be dependent on no one*." The point here is not that our work will save anyone. The point is that if we live and work well, obstacles will be removed. In other words, good, honest work is not the saving Gospel of God, but a crooked Christian car salesmen is a blemish on the Gospel and puts a roadblock in the way of seeing the beauty of Christ. And sloth may be a greater stumbling block than crime. Should Christians be known in their offices as the ones you go to if you have a problem, but not the ones to go to with a complex professional issue? It doesn't have to be either-or. The biblical mandate is: "Whatever you do, work heartily, as for the Lord and not for men" (Colossians 3:23; cf. Ephesians 6:7).

So the third way we make much of God in our secular work is by having such high standards of excellence and such integrity and such manifest goodwill that we put no obstacles in the way of the Gospel but rather call attention to the all-satisfying beauty of Christ. When we adorn the Gospel with our work, we are not wasting our lives. And when we call to mind that the adornment itself (our God-dependent, God-shaped, God-exalting work) was purchased for us by the blood of Christ, and that the beauty we adorn is itself the Gospel of Christ's death, then all our tender adornment becomes a boasting in the cross.

4. We make much of Christ in our secular work by earning enough money to keep us from depending on others, while focusing on the helpfulness of our work rather than financial rewards.

God intended from the beginning that satisfying work would provide for our needs. God worked at the beginning (Genesis 2:2), and the humans he created in his image would work. Before sin entered the world, that work would be without futility and frustration. It would unite beautifully with God's abundant provision to meet every need. It would make the earth subject to man's material needs without ruining the earth (Genesis 1:28). At the beginning, the homestead of man was a garden of fruit trees, not a hard field to be plowed and planted. "Out of the ground the LORD God made to spring up every tree that is pleasant to the sight and good for food" (Genesis 2:9). Not only that, "a river flowed out of Eden to water the garden" (verse 10).

Happy Work Before the Fall; Then
Sweating and Fretting

In this all-supplying paradise God said, at first, "there was no man to work the ground" (verse 5). Then he made man from the ground, and, in his creation, Adam became a son working with his Father in the stewardship of creation. The essence of work was not sustenance of life. God gave himself as the sustainer. Man was free, not *from* work, but *in* work, to be creative without the anxiety of providing food and clothing.

What changed with the entrance of sin into the world was not that man had to work, but that work became hard with the futility and frustration of the fallen creation. The Lord said to Adam:

> *Because you have listened to the voice of your wife and have eaten of the tree of which I commanded you,* "You shall not eat of it," *cursed is the ground because of you;* in pain you shall eat of it all the days of your life; thorns and thistles it shall bring forth for you; *and you shall eat the plants of the field.* By the sweat of your face you shall eat bread, *till you return to the ground. (Genesis 3:17-19, emphasis added)*

When man and woman chose to be self-reliant and rejected God's fatherly guidance and provision, God subjected them to the very thing they chose: self-reliance. From now on, he says, if you eat, it will be because you toil and sweat. So they were driven from the garden of happy work to the ground of anxious toil. The curse under which we live today is not that we must work. The curse is that, in our work, we struggle with weariness and frustration and calamities and anxiety. And all this is doubly burdensome because now by this very toil we must keep ourselves alive. "In toil you shall eat of the ground. . . . In the sweat of your face you shall eat bread."

Christ Took the Curse on Himself, and
We Are Being Freed

But hasn't Christ come to lift the curse from his people? Yes. "Christ redeemed us from the curse of the law by becoming a curse for us—for it is written, 'Cursed is everyone who is hanged on a tree'" (Galatians 3:13). However, the curse is not lifted totally all at once. God saves us in stages. Christ delivered a mortal blow to evil when he died for sin and rose again. But not every enemy is yet put under his feet. For example, death is part of the curse we still experience. Christ conquered death for his people, but only partly now. We still die, but the "sting" of death, the hopelessness of death, is removed because our sins are forgiven in Christ and he is risen (1 Corinthians 15:54-55)!

Similarly, we must still work hard to provide for our needs. Christ says, "Do not be anxious about your life, what you will eat or what you will drink, nor about your body, what you will put on. . . . Your heavenly Father knows that you need them all. But seek first the kingdom of God and his righteousness, and all these things will be added to you" (Matthew 6:25, 32-33). He says, "Come to me, all who labor and are heavy laden, and I will give you rest" (Matthew 11:28). He says, "Be steadfast, immovable, always abounding in the work of the Lord, knowing that in the Lord your labor is not in vain" (1 Corinthians 15:58). In other words, God does not want his children to be burdened with the frustration and futility and depressing weariness of work. That much of the curse he aims to lift from us even in this age.

Paradise Is Not Here Yet

But just as death will be a reality to the end of this age, so must we work in this fallen age against many obstacles that often make work hard. Not yet may we return to paradise and pick fruit in someone else's garden. That's the mistake they made at Thessalonica. Some were quitting their jobs and being idle because they thought that Christ would come very soon. Paradise was at hand. So Paul wrote to them, "If anyone is not willing to work, let him not eat. For we hear that some of you walk in idleness, not busy at work, but busybodies. Now such persons we command and encourage in the Lord Jesus Christ to do their work quietly and to earn their own living" (2 Thessalonians 3:10-12). Able-bodied people who choose to live in idleness and eat the fruit of another's sweat are in rebellion against God's design. If we can, we should earn our own living.

How then do Christians make much of Christ in working "to earn their own living"? First, by conforming willingly to God's design for this age. It is an act of obedience that honors his authority. Second, by removing stumbling blocks from unbelievers who would regard the lazy dependence of Christians on others as an evidence that our God is not worthy of following. "Work with your hands . . . so that you may live properly before outsiders and be dependent on no one" (1 Thessalonians 4:11-12). We honor God by earning our living because this clears the way for non-Christians to see Christ for who he really is. Aimless, unproductive Christians contradict the creative, purposeful, powerful, merciful God we love. They waste their lives.

Do Not Labor for the Food That Perishes

Third, we make much of God by earning our own living when we focus not on financial profit but on the benefit our product or service brings to society. This is paradoxical. I am saying, yes, we should earn enough money to meet our needs. But, no, we should not make *that* the primary focus of why we work. One of the most striking things Jesus ever said was, *"Do not labor for the food that perishes*, but for the food that endures to eternal life, which the Son of Man will give to you" (John 6:27). Do not labor for the food that perishes! "The food that perishes" simply means all ordinary food and provision. So this is striking! It seems to say the exact opposite of what I am saying. What does he mean?

We know from all we have seen so far that Jesus does not mean it is wrong to earn your own living and eat your own bread. Evidently then, he means that when we work for the food that perishes, there should be a significant sense in which we are not working for that food, but for something more. In other words, don't focus on mere material things in your work. Don't labor merely with a view to the perishable things you can buy with your earnings. Work with an eye not mainly to your money, but your usefulness. Work with a view to benefiting people with what you make or do.

Christ has lifted the curse of work. He has replaced anxious toil with trust in God's promise to supply our needs (Philippians 4:19) and has thus awakened in us a different passion in our work. We turn with joy to the call of Jesus: Seek the kingdom of God first and his righteousness, and the food that perishes will be added to you. So don't labor for the food that perishes. Labor to love people and honor God. Think of new ways that your work can bless people. Stop thinking mainly of profitability, and think mainly of how helpful your product or service can become.

Do Your Business Dealings but Stay Free from Them
How do you get up in the morning and go to work *not* for the food that perishes—not mainly for the profit? This is really a

spiritual discovery, attained through much prayer and longing. My words of explanation won't make it happen. But maybe the Holy Spirit will use these words to advance your quest. Paul said in 1 Corinthians 7:30-31 that since we live in a time of great urgency, "those who buy [should buy] as though they had no goods, and those who deal with the world as though they had no dealings with it." I think this is another way of saying, yes, labor, but do not labor for the food that perishes. Go ahead and purchase, but act as though you have no goods. Do your business dealings, but stay free from them. The financial outcome of these dealings is not your life.

Say You Are a Stockbroker

Suppose you are a Christian stockbroker and have watched the market tumble. What it means to you not to labor for the food that perishes is that your true life is not jeopardized. Your peace and joy are not destroyed. Your resolve to do the best you can for your clients remains the same—even if you advise them to get out of the market and use their money a different way for God's glory. You are not working for the food that perishes. Your goal is to enjoy Christ's being exalted in the way you work. Jesus said, "I have food to eat that you do not know about. . . . My food is to do the will of him who sent me and to accomplish his work" (John 4:32-34). None of us in our vocations should aim mainly at the food that perishes—leave that to the Lord. We should aim instead to do the will of him who sent us. And his will is that we treasure him above all else and live like it.

The Christian stockbroker will say in the face of a falling market, "The main food I want from this job is still there. I am hungry above all to pass this test of faith and have a deep restfulness in the goodness and power of Christ. I am hungry to enjoy his name being esteemed as others see my demeanor and my integrity and give Christ glory." And to that end he labors for the food that endures to eternal life. He labors, rising early for prayer and meditation and holding Christ near to his heart all day. In that security he thinks of the good of others and serves them. That is a wonder, not a wasted life.

Jesus calls us to be aliens and exiles in the world. Not by taking us out of the world, but by changing, at the root, how we view the world and how we do our work in it. If we simply work to earn a living—if we labor for the bread that perishes—we will waste our lives. But if we labor with the sweet assurance that God will supply all our needs—that Christ died to purchase every undeserved blessing—then all our labor will be a labor of love and a boasting only in the cross.

5. We make much of Christ in our secular work by earning money with the desire to use our money to make others glad in God.

Everything I said in Chapter 7 assumed that we had money to use in a radical way to show that Christ and not money is our Treasure. But money does not grow on trees; we work for it. We provide some service or make some product that others will pay for. So my point here is that, as we work, we should dream of how to use our excess money to make others glad in God. Of course, we should use *all* our money to make others glad in God, in the sense that our whole life has this aim. But the point here is that our secular work can become a great God-exalting blessing to the world if we aim to take the earnings we don't need for ourselves (and we *need* far less than we think) and meet the needs of others in the name of Jesus.

The Able-Bodied Earners Help the Victims of Loss

God clearly tells us that we should work to provide the needs of those who can't meet their own needs. It's true that everyone should work if he can, and that, in general, if you work you will have what you need. "Whoever works his land will have plenty of bread" (Proverbs 12:11). But this general rule is not absolute. Drought may strike your farm; thieves may steal what you've earned; disability may end your earning power. All that is part of the curse that sin brought into the world. But God, in his mercy, wills that the work of the able-bodied supply the needs of the helpless, especially in hard times.

Three passages of Scripture make this plain. In 1 Timothy 5:8 Paul speaks to children and grandchildren regarding the aged widows: "If anyone does not provide for his relatives, and especially for members of his own household, he has denied the faith and is worse than an unbeliever." In Acts 20:35 Paul refers to his own manual labor and then says, "In all things I have shown you that by working hard in this way we must help the weak and remember the words of the Lord Jesus, how he himself said, 'It is more blessed to give than to receive.'" Then in Ephesians 4:28 Paul doesn't settle for saying, "Don't steal, work!" He says, "Let the thief no longer steal, but rather let him labor, doing honest work with his own hands, *so that he may have something to share with anyone in need.*" You can steal to have. Or you can work to have. Or you can work to have to give. When the third option comes from joy in God's goodness, it makes him look great in the world.

6. We make much of Christ in our secular work by treating the web of relationships it creates as a gift of God to be loved by sharing the Gospel and by practical deeds of help.

I put this last not because it is least important but because some who put it first never say anything else about the importance of secular work. I have made this mistake myself. Personal evangelism is so important that it is easy to think of it as the only important thing in life. But we have seen that the Bible puts a lot of emphasis on adorning the Gospel, not merely saying the Gospel. But now I want to say that *speaking* the good news of

Christ is part of why God put you in your job. He has woven you into the fabric of others' lives so that you will tell them the Gospel. Without this, all our adorning behavior may lack the one thing that could make it life-giving.

The Christian's calling includes making his or her mouth a fountain of life. "The mouth of the righteous is a fountain of life" (Proverbs 10:11). The link with eternal life is faith in Jesus Christ. No nice feelings about you as a good employee will save anyone. People must know the Gospel, which is the power of God unto eternal life (Romans 1:16). "Faith comes from hearing, and hearing through the word of Christ" (Romans 10:17).

The early church was a "gospelling" band of people. They spoke the Gospel. When the believers were driven out of Jerusalem because of persecution after Stephen's martyrdom, they "went about preaching the word"—literally, "evangelizing or gospelling the word" (Acts 8:4). The Gospel was on their lips in all their new relationships. Their self-identity was "proclaimers": "You are a chosen race, a royal priesthood, a holy nation, a people for his own possession, *that you may proclaim* the excellencies of him who called you out of darkness into his marvelous light" (1 Peter 2:9). Freely they had received. Freely they gave.

They were moved by the words of Jesus concerning the value of a single human life: "What does it profit a man to gain the whole world and forfeit his life? For what can a man give in return for his life?" (Mark 8:36-37). They felt the weight of what C. S. Lewis spoke twenty centuries later when he pondered the relationship between winning one soul to Christ, on the one hand, and the value of his own vocation as an Oxford scholar of English Literature on the other hand:

> The Christian will take literature a little less seriously than the cultured Pagan. . . . The unbeliever is always apt to make a kind of religion of his aesthetic experiences . . . and he com-

monly wishes to maintain his superiority to the great mass of mankind who turn to books for mere recreation. But the Christian knows from the outset that *the salvation of a single soul is more important than the production or preservation of all the epics and tragedies in the world*: and as for superiority, he knows that the vulgar since they include most of the poor probably include most of the superiors.[4]

The point is not that Lewis quit his work and became a full-time evangelist, nor that you should. The point is that he saw the meaning of his work in proper perspective and knew that more than one thing gave it significance. To each of the five ways that we have mentioned above, Lewis would add that his vocation created a web of relationships in which he could speak the Gospel. Once when he was criticized for oversimplifying the Gospel, he responded to his critic:

[He] would be a more helpful critic if he advised a cure as well as asserting many diseases. How does he himself do such work? What methods, and with what success, does he employ when he is trying to convert the great mass of storekeepers, lawyers, realtors, morticians, policemen and artisans who surround him in his own city?[5]

Perhaps one other thing should be mentioned in regard to the relationships created by where we live and work. For many of you the move toward missions and deeds of mercy will not be a move away from your work but with your work to another, more needy, less-reached part of the world. Christians should seriously ask not only what their vocation is, but where it should be lived out. We should not assume that teachers and carpenters and computer programmers and managers and CPAs and doctors and pilots should do their work in America. That very vocation may be better used in a country that is otherwise hard to get into, or in a place where poverty makes access to the Gospel difficult. In this way the web of relationships created by our work is not only strategic but intentional.

CONCLUSION

In conclusion, secular work is not a waste when we make much of Christ from 8 to 5. God's will in this age is that his people be scattered like salt and light in all legitimate vocations. His aim is to be known, because knowing him is life and joy. He does not call us out of the world. He does not remove the need to work. He does not destroy society and culture. Through his scattered saints he spreads a passion for his supremacy in all things for the joy of all peoples. If you work like the world, you will waste your life, no matter how rich you get. But if your work creates a web of redemptive relationships and becomes an adornment for the Gospel of the glory of Christ, your satisfaction will last forever and God will be exalted in your joy.

NOTES

1   Martin Luther, "An Open Letter to the Christian Nobility," in *Three Treatises* (Philadelphia: Fortress, 1960), 14-17. See Gene Edward Veith, Jr., *God at Work: Your Christian Vocation in All of Life* (Wheaton, Ill.: Crossway, 2002) for an exposition for laypeople of Luther's doctrine of vocation. See also Os Guinness, *The Call: Finding and Fulfilling the Central Purpose of Your Life* (Nashville: Word, 1998), and Paul Helm, *Callings: The Gospel in the World* (Edinburgh: Banner of Truth Trust, 1998).

2   Cecil F. Alexander, "All Things Bright and Beautiful" (1848).

3   Jonathan Edwards, "Thoughts Concerning the Revival," in *The Great Awakening, The Works of Jonathan Edwards*, Vol. 4 (New Haven, Conn.: Yale University Press, 1972), 340.

4   C. S. Lewis, "Christianity and Literature," in *Christian Reflections* (Grand Rapids, Mich.: Eerdmans, 1967), 10.

5   C. S. Lewis, "Rejoinder to Dr. Pittenger," in *God in the Dock: Essays on Theology and Ethics* (Grand Rapids, Mich.: Eerdmans, 1970), 183.

CHAPTER 9
THE MAJESTY OF CHRIST IN MISSIONS AND MERCY—A PLEA TO THIS GENERATION

*G*od is closing in on some of you. He is like the "Hound of Heaven" who means to make you far happier in some dangerous and dirty work. Missionaries and ministers of mercy don't come from nowhere. They come from people like you, stunned by the glory of God and stopped in your tracks. Sometimes it happens when you are going in exactly the opposite direction.

HOW GOD CAUGHT ADONIRAM JUDSON FOR BURMA

That's the way it was with Adoniram Judson, the first overseas missionary from America, who sailed with his wife at age twenty-three on February 17, 1812. They had been married twelve days. He spent the rest of his life, until 1850, "suffering yet always rejoicing" to bring Burma under the sway of Christ and make the people glad in God forever. But first God had to turn him around, and he did it in a way that so stunned Judson, he never forgot the providence of God in his conversion.[1]

The son of a pastor, he was a brilliant boy. His mother taught him to read in one week when he was three to surprise his father when he came home from a trip.[2] When he was sixteen he entered Rhode Island College (later Brown University) as a sophomore and graduated at the top of his class three years later in 1807.

THE DETOUR FROM GOD

What his godly parents did not know was that Adoniram was being lured away from the faith by a fellow student named Jacob Eames who was a Deist.[3] By the time Judson's college career was finished, he had no Christian faith. He kept this concealed from his parents until his twentieth birthday, August 9, 1808, when he broke their hearts with his announcement that he had no faith and that he wanted to write for the theater and intended to go to New York, which he did six days later on a horse his father gave him as part of his inheritance.

It did not prove to be the life of his dreams. He attached himself to some strolling players and, as he said later, lived "a reckless, vagabond life, finding lodgings where he could, and bilking the landlord where he found opportunity."[4] The disgust with what he found there was the beginning of several remarkable providences. God was closing in on Adoniram Judson.

He went to visit his Uncle Ephraim in Sheffield but found there instead "a pious young man" who amazed him by being firm in his Christian convictions without being "austere and dictatorial."[5] Strange that he should find this young man there instead of the uncle he sought.

THE UNFORGETTABLE NIGHT

The next night he stayed in a small village inn where he had never been before. The innkeeper apologized that his sleep might be interrupted because there was a man critically ill in the next room. Through the night Judson heard comings and goings and low voices and groans and gasps. It bothered him to think that the man next to him may not be prepared to die. He wondered about himself and had terrible thoughts of his own dying. He felt foolish because good Deists weren't supposed to have these struggles.

When he was leaving in the morning he asked if the man next door was better. "He is dead," said the innkeeper. Judson was struck with the finality of it all. On his way out he asked, "Do you know who he was?" "Oh yes. Young man from the college in Providence. Name was Eames, Jacob Eames."[6]

Judson could hardly move. He stayed there for hours pondering death and eternity. If his friend Eames were right, then this was a meaningless event. But Judson could not believe it: "That hell should open in that country inn and snatch Jacob Eames, his dearest friend and guide, from the next bed—this could not, simply could not, be pure coincidence."[7] God was real. And he was pursuing Adoniram Judson. God knew the man he wanted to reach the Burmese people.

ALIVE TO CHRIST AND DEAD TO AMERICA

Judson's conversion was not immediate. But now it was sure. God was on his trail, like the apostle Paul on the Damascus road, and there was no escape. There were months of struggle. He entered Andover Seminary in October 1808 and in December made solemn dedication of himself to God. On June 28, 1809, Judson presented himself to the Congregationalists for missionary service in the East.

He met Ann that same day and fell in love. After knowing Ann Hasseltine for one month he declared his intention to become a suitor. He knew that the life he was about to embrace would not only be dangerous and dirty, but also distant. He never expected to return to America. He did only once, thirty-three years later, then never again. Ann went with him and died in Burma. Here is the letter Judson wrote to her father asking for her partnership in missions:

> I have now to ask, whether you can consent to part with your daughter early next spring, to see her no more in this world; whether you can consent to her departure, and her subjection to the hardships and sufferings of missionary life; whether you can consent to her exposure to the dangers of the ocean, to the fatal influence of the southern climate of India; to every kind of want and distress; to degradation, insult, persecution, and perhaps a violent death. Can you consent to all this, for the sake of him who left his heavenly home, and died for her and for you; for the sake of perishing, immortal souls; for the sake of Zion, and the glory of God? Can you consent to all this, in hope of soon meeting your daughter in the world of glory, with the crown of righteousness, brightened with the acclamations of praise which shall redound to her Savior from heathens saved, through her means, from eternal woe and despair?[8]

Her father let her decide. She said yes.

God does not call us to ease, but to faithful joy. He is closing in on some of you, smiling and with tears in his eyes, knowing how much of himself he is going to show you—and how much it will cost. As I write, I pray that you will not turn away.

PITY FOR PEOPLE AND A PASSION FOR CHRIST ARE ONE

If you have pity for perishing people and a passion for the reputation of Christ, you must care about world missions. One of the burdens of this book is to show what life looks like when you believe that you dare not choose between the motives to love people and glorify Christ. They are not separate motives. Acting on one includes acting on the other. Thus, if your aim is to love people, you will lay down your life to make them eternally glad in God. And if your aim is to glorify Christ, who is God incarnate, you will also lay down your life to make people eternally happy in God.

The reason for this is that any good-hearted goal, without the desire to give people eternal joy in God, is condemnation with a kind face. Love always wants what is best for the needy, and what's best is enjoying God fully and forever. Similarly, any effort to honor Christ that does not aim to make him the all-satisfying Treasure of God's treasonous subjects is complicity in the revolt. God is only praised where he is prized. We pay our tribute to him when he is a Treasure to us. You cannot love man or honor God without doing both. This single passion—to see that Christ be glorified as perishing people become eternally satisfied in him—drives the great global enterprise we call world missions.

IF YOU COME WITH NO INTEREST OR KNOWLEDGE

Not everybody comes to this chapter with a clear and driving passion for the glory of Christ among the unreached peoples of the world. Most of us are pretty parochial and ethnocentric and narrow, and even sometimes self-centered and racist, in our way of life. We hardly ever even think about the global, multinational, multiethnic, multi-linguistic cause of God, and what God's passion and purposes are for Guinea and Indonesia and Tanzania and Thailand and Kazakhstan and Uzbekistan and Turkey and Czechoslovakia and China and Siberia and Japan and Cameroon and Myanmar and the Somali or the Hmong or the Dakota or the Ojibwa of Minnesota.

So I don't assume that you come to this chapter with a clear and resounding interest in the really great news of the world—

which the media never report—namely, the spread of Christian truth and faith among the peoples of the world on the way to a God-wrought consummation that will make all of world history look like what it really is—a brief prelude to the everlasting, all-glorious kingdom of Christ. I don't assume you come with your heart enthralled with God's great global purpose. So I simply want to let God tell you, in his own words, about his priorities.

> *All the ends of the earth shall remember and turn to the* LORD, *and all the families of the nations shall worship before you. For kingship belongs to the* LORD, *and he rules over the nations. (Psalm 22:27-28)*

Then there are *Old Testament prayers*:

> *Let the peoples praise you, O God; let all the peoples praise you! Let the nations be glad and sing for joy. (Psalm 67:3-4)*

Then there are *Old Testament commands*:

> *Declare his glory among the nations, his marvelous works among all the peoples! . . . Say among the nations, "The* LORD *reigns." (Psalm 96:3, 10)*

Then there is *the great New Testament Commission from the risen Christ*:

> *Jesus came and said to them, "All authority in heaven and on earth has been given to me. Go therefore and make disciples of all nations, baptizing them in the name of the Father and of the Son and of the Holy Spirit, teaching them to observe all that I have commanded you. And behold, I am with you always, to the end of the age." (Matthew 28:18-20)*

Then there is *the apostle Paul's great life of utter dedication to this mission*:

> I make it my ambition to preach the gospel, not where Christ has already been named, lest I build on someone else's foundation, but as it is written, "Those who have never been told of him will see, and those who have never heard will understand." (Romans 15:20-21)

Then there is *the magnificent picture of the final outcome of God's purposes in history*:

> And they sang a new song, saying, "Worthy are you [O Christ] to take the scroll and to open its seals, for you were slain, and by your blood you ransomed people for God from every tribe and language and people and nation, and you have made them a kingdom and priests to our God, and they shall reign on the earth." (Revelation 5:9-10)

A SUMMARY STATEMENT OF FAITH ON MISSIONS

From these and many other Scriptures, I have been impelled over the years to think and preach and write about Christ's great global purpose called missions. Several years ago the elders of our church drafted a statement of faith to guide us in the education of our apprentices and in the selection of new elders. Paragraph 13 of that document summarizes our sense of what missions is:

> We believe that the commission given by the Lord Jesus to make disciples of all nations is binding on His Church to the end of the age. This task is to proclaim the Gospel to every tribe and tongue and people and nation, baptizing them, teaching them the words and ways of the Lord, and gather-

ing them into churches able to fulfill their Christian calling among their own people. The ultimate aim of world missions is that God would create, by His Word, worshippers who glorify His name through glad-hearted faith and obedience. Missions exists because worship doesn't. When this age is over, and the countless millions of the redeemed fall on their faces before the throne of God, missions will be no more. It is a temporary necessity. But worship abides forever. Worship, therefore, is the fuel and the goal of missions.[9]

EVEN CIVILIANS LOVE TO FOLLOW THE TRIUMPHS ON THE FRONT LINES

This is the big picture. Christ came and died and rose again in order to gather a joyful, countless company for his name from all the peoples of the world. This is what every Christian should dream about. I say this carefully, in view of what I wrote in Chapter 8 about secular vocations. It is crucial that millions of Christians fulfill their life calling in secular jobs, just as it is crucial that during wartime the entire fabric of life and culture not unravel. But during wartime, even the millions of civilians love to get news from the front lines. They love to hear of the triumphs of the troops. They dream about the day when war will be no more. So it is with Christians. All of us should dream about this. We should love to hear how the advance of King Jesus is faring. We should love to hear of gospel triumphs as Christ plants his church among peoples held for centuries by alien powers of darkness.

This is God's design in world history—that people from all nations and tribes and languages come to worship and treasure Christ above all things. Or as Paul put it in Romans 15:9, "that the Gentiles [all the peoples] might glorify God for his mercy." There can be no weary resignation, no cowardly retreat, and no merciless contentment among Christ's people while he is disowned among thousands of unreached peoples. Every Christian (who loves people and honors Christ) must care about this.

THE INADEQUACY OF THE BATBOY'S PERSPECTIVE

Someone might say, "But isn't the Gospel about finding forgiveness of my sins and getting the hope of eternal life and being filled with the Spirit of holiness and being changed into the image of Jesus so that I am a better mom or dad or son or daughter or friend or employer or citizen?" The answer, of course, is yes. But if that is all we focus on in our walk with God, we miss the big picture. We miss the bigger point of it all. We are like batboys at Yankee Stadium who think the great point of the World Series is to hand the players a bat.

So I urge you in the name of Jesus to wake up, and enlarge your heart, and stretch your mind, and spread your wings. Mount up above your limited life—yes, a very important life, which God does not diminish—and see the great and thrilling big picture of God's global purposes for the history of the world that cannot fail. "My counsel shall stand," says the Lord, "and I will accomplish all my purpose" (Isaiah 46:10). "At the name of Jesus every knee [will] bow, in heaven and on earth and under the earth, and every tongue confess that Jesus Christ is Lord, to the glory of God the Father" (Philippians 2:10-11). "This gospel of the kingdom will be proclaimed throughout the whole world as a testimony to all nations, and then the end will come" (Matthew 24:14).

DON'T TAKE OFFENSE—JOIN THE JOYFUL PARTNERSHIP

And as God gives you wings to rise up and see the world the way he sees it, many of you, I pray, will be loosened from your pres-ent situation—job, neighborhood, state, nation, plan—and be called to a direct engagement in this great historic, global purpose of God as a goer and not only a sender. Let no one who is devoted to local ministry or to crucial secular engagement take offense at this plea. Rather rejoice. You are free to stay or free to go. Many of you must stay. Your staying is crucial for God's purposes where you are, and it is crucial for his purposes where you are not, but where others may go. There is no need for guilt or resentment. There is great need for joyful partnership.

Those of you who stay—the senders—should keep this remarkable fact in mind: Foreign missions is a validation of *all* ministries of mercy at home because it exports them abroad. Planting the church in an unreached people means planting the base of operations for all the mercy Jesus commanded for the poor. If we don't let our light shine before the people at home "so that they may see [our] good works and give glory to [our] Father who is in heaven" (Matthew 5:16), what kind of obedience will we export to the nations? The Great Commission includes the words, "teaching them to observe all that I [Jesus] have commanded you" (Matthew 28:20). And what did he command? He told the story of the desperate wounded man and the good Samaritan who "showed him mercy," and then said to all of us, "You go, and do likewise" (Luke 10:37).

MERCY AT HOME MAKES MISSIONS CREDIBLE

The people who stay in the homeland are surrounded by need. We only need eyes to see and hearts that can't walk by on the other side. This challenge is not separate from the challenge of missions. Showing practical mercy to the poor displays the beauty of Christ at home and makes the exportation of the Christian faith credible. We are hypocrites to pretend enthusiasm for overseas ministry while neglecting the miseries at home. There was something wrong with the priest and the Levite in the story of the good Samaritan, who had their distant religious aims but were not moved by suffering close at hand where they would have to get their own hands dirty. Ministries of mercy close at hand validate the authenticity of our distant concerns.

Foreign missions and hometown mercy are linked in the very nature of the Gospel that we are to send to the nations. The heart of the Gospel is this: "Though [Christ] was rich, yet for your sake he became poor, so that you by his poverty might become rich" (2 Corinthians 8:9). The salvation we savor for ourselves and send to others is a ministry of God's mercy to the poor, which includes all of us. We owe our lives to God's commitment to missions and mercy. He came a long way to help us, and his help includes every kind of help we need. And he got dirty doing it. In fact he got killed. This merciful suffering is the *purchase* and the *path* of our salvation. "Christ also suffered *for you*, leaving you an *example*, so that you might follow in his steps" (1 Peter 2:21). Missions and mercy are inextricable because the very Gospel we take to the nations models and mandates mercy to the poor at home.

WARFIELD'S DEVASTATING COMPARISON

I have never read a better statement of this connection than the following quote from B. B. Warfield, a teacher at Princeton Seminary who died in 1921. He answers some of the niggling questions about ministry to the poor by comparing it to Christ's ministry to us.

> Now dear Christians, some of you pray night and day to be branches of the true Vine; you pray to be made all over in the image of Christ. If so, you must be like him in giving . . . "though he was rich, yet for our sakes he became poor" . . . Objection 1. "My money is my own." Answer: Christ might have said, "My blood is my own, my life is my own" . . . then where should we have been? Objection 2. "The poor are undeserving." Answer: Christ might have said, "They

are wicked rebels . . . shall I lay down my life for these? I will give to the good angels." But no, he left the ninety-nine, and came after the lost. He gave his blood for the undeserving. Objection 3. "The poor may abuse it." Answer: Christ might have said the same; yea, with far greater truth. Christ knew that thousands would trample his blood under their feet; that most would despise it; that many would make it an excuse for sinning more; yet he gave his own blood. Oh, my dear Christians! If you would be like Christ, give much, give often, give freely, to the vile and poor, the thankless and the undeserving. Christ is glorious and happy and so will you be. It is not your money I want, but your happiness. Remember his own word, "It is more blessed to give than to receive."[10]

Just as there is a partnership between the Gospel itself and mercy to the nearby poor, so there is a wonderful partnership between Christians *being* the merciful church at home and Christians *planting* the merciful church abroad. Neither is a wasted life. Indeed the authenticity of each depends much on the authenticity of the other. It is inauthentic to presume to send what we don't have. And it is inauthentic to have a treasure and not send it.

THE ROOTS OF THE STUDENT VOLUNTEER MOVEMENT

The joyful partnership between ministering laypeople at home and missionaries abroad has happened before, and it can happen again. In the first decades of the twentieth century, the Student Volunteer Movement exploded on the American scene with immense missionary impact. It was remarkable for the number of missionaries sent and for the depth and breadth of the laymen who supported it. It was a magnificent partnership.

The roots of the Student Volunteer Movement (SVM) went back as far as the famous Haystack Prayer Meeting in 1806 in Massachusetts. A spiritual awakening stirred the students of

Williams College and prompted a small band of young men to devote themselves to prayer twice a week by the Hoosack River. They focused on the spiritual welfare of the other students. In August 1806, they were caught in a thunderstorm on their way home and took refuge under the edges of a chewed-out haystack. They used the time to continue praying. This time they pleaded for the awakening of foreign missionary interest among the students.

One of them, Samuel Mills, urged the little group to consider their own willingness to be missionaries. To feel the weight of this moment, we have to remember that at this time in American history not one foreign missionary had left the shores of America. There were no missionary societies. Churches, by and large, had no vision for the unreached peoples across the dangerous oceans. There was, as many say today, plenty to do at home. Which was true! But this little band of praying students could no longer be content with an American church whose heart did not burn with love for unreached peoples and with zeal for the glory of God among the nations. They could no longer be satisfied with a church that sent no foreign missionaries. Against all this spiritual, historical, and structural inertia, God enabled them to break through.

"THE BRETHREN" WERE BORN

Praying under the haystack they dedicated themselves to missionary service. "It was from this haystack meeting that the foreign missionary movement of the churches of the United States had an initial impulse."[11] That September, the group formed the "Society of the Brethren" to strengthen their resolve to give themselves to missionary service. Samuel Mills spread "The Brethren" vision as he studied at Yale and then at Andover Seminary. He had transferred to Andover to be a part of what God was doing there under the student leadership of Adoniram

Judson. This group of "Brethren" at Andover gave the impetus to the first American mission agency (the American Board of Commissioners for Foreign Missions); and from this group were sent the first overseas American missionaries in 1812.

THE STUDENT VOLUNTEER MOVEMENT IS BORN

In 1846, Royal Wilder went to India under this first American Board of Commissioners. He returned in 1877 for health reasons and settled in Princeton. There his son, Robert, formed the "Princeton Foreign Missionary Society." The prayers of this group gave rise to a crucial gathering called by D. L. Moody at Mount Hermon, Massachusetts, in the summer of 1886. Two hundred and fifty-one students gathered for a month-long Bible conference. After a compelling address by pastor A. T. Pierson on behalf of world missions, a hundred of these students volunteered for overseas service. The spirit of this event gripped the student world. During the school year 1886-1887, Robert Wilder and John Forman traveled to 167 campuses to spread the vision. The formal organization of the Student Volunteer Movement happened two years later with John R. Mott as its chairman.

The purpose, as Mott expressed it, had five parts:

> The fivefold purpose of the Student Volunteer Movement is to lead students to a thorough consideration of the claims of foreign missions upon them personally as a lifework; to foster this purpose by guiding students who become volunteers in their study and activity for missions until they come under the immediate direction of the Mission Boards; to unite all volunteers in a common, organized, aggressive movement; to secure a sufficient number of well-qualified volunteers to meet the demands of the various Mission Boards; and to create and maintain an intelligent, sympathetic and active interest in foreign missions on the part of students who are to remain at home in order to ensure the strong backing of

the missionary enterprise by their advocacy, their gifts and their prayers.[12]

"The growth of the SVM in the following three decades was nothing short of phenomenal."[13] The rallying cry was, "Evangelization of the world in this generation." By 1891 there were 6,200 student volunteers who had signed a statement that read, "It is my purpose, if God permit, to become a foreign missionary." Of these, 321 had already sailed for overseas service. The peak year of the SVM was 1920, when 2,738 students signed the pledge card and 6,890 attended the quadrennial convention. "By 1945, at the most conservative estimate, 20,500 students . . . who had signed the declaration, reached the field."[14]

THE STUDENT FLAME IGNITED BUSINESSES AND CHURCHES

Many things are remarkable about this movement, and full of instruction and inspiration for our generation a hundred years later. For example, the Student Volunteer Movement ignited not just students but the laymen of the churches. J. Campbell White, the first secretary of the Layman's Missionary Movement, wrote in 1909, "During the last twenty years the missionary spirit has had a marvelous development among the colleges of the United States and Canada . . . leading thousands of strong men and women to live with a dominating missionary life purpose."[15] Attracted by this zeal, a young businessman attended the 1906 SVM convention in Nashville. He thought to himself, *If the laymen of North America could see the world as these students are seeing it, they would rise up in their strength and provide all the funds needed for the enterprise.*[16] At a prayer meeting of businessmen on November 15, 1906, in New York, the Layman's Missionary Movement was born.

Its stated aim was "investigation, agitation and organization; the investigation by laymen of missionary conditions, the agitation of laymen of an adequate missionary policy, and the organization of laymen to co-operate with the ministers and Missionary Boards in enlisting the whole Church in its supreme work of saving the world."[17]

THE GIFT OF PASSIONATE LEADERS

Just as God had prepared extraordinary leadership for the SVM in Robert Wilder, Robert Speer, and John R. Mott, so he raised up leaders for the Layman's Missionary Movement who spoke with such prophetic power that thousands of laymen caught the vision for God's global purposes. The leader of the movement was not a missionary and not a pastor. He was a businessman. The partnership that emerged between students, who were going, and businessmen, who were sending, was profound, because there were God-centered visionary leaders in both groups. Both were moved by the same passion not to waste their lives. You can hear it in almost every sentence that J. Campbell White wrote:

> Most men are not satisfied with the permanent output of their lives. Nothing can wholly satisfy the life of Christ within his followers except the adoption of Christ's purpose toward the world he came to redeem. Fame, pleasure and riches are but husks and ashes in contrast with the boundless and abiding joy of working with God for the fulfillment of his eternal plans. The men who are putting everything into Christ's undertaking are getting out of life its sweetest and most priceless rewards.[18]

SENDERS ARE UNASHAMED TO EMBRACE
THE CAUSE OF GOING

Again, this is not a contradiction of what I wrote about the value of secular work in Chapter 8. The point is that, in a war, no matter how valuable the civilian work is in itself, everyone longs for his life to count also for the distant war effort, where enemy lines are being breached. Laypeople, pastors, churches—all of us who stay behind—will find the "sweetest and most priceless rewards" as we enlarge our hearts to embrace not only the needs close to home, but also the hard and unreached places of the world.

These businessmen from a hundred years ago saw their secular calling and their missionary vision as an integrated whole. The way J. Campbell White articulated the vision of the movement gave the businessmen categories for understanding the unity of life under the lordship of Christ. He said:

> This movement makes the largest possible demands upon men. It strives simply to voice to them God's call for a life whose dominant purpose is to establish the reign of Christ in human relationships. . . . It reminds them . . . that selfishness is suicidal while service of others brings to the soul the supremest possible satisfaction.[19]

THE STARTLING EFFECT ON THE CHURCH THEN, BUT WHAT ABOUT TODAY?

White showed his generation that a passion for missions was not only the way to save the world, but also to save the church:

> The effort to evangelize the world presents the speediest and surest methods of saving the Church. Our material resources are so stupendous that we are in danger of coming to trust in riches rather than in God. "If a man is growing large in wealth, nothing but constant giving can keep him from growing small in soul." The evangelization of the world is the only enterprise large enough and important enough to provide an adequate outlet for the Church's wealth.[20]

This is still true. Missions is not only crucial for the life of the world. It is crucial for the life of the church. We will perish with our wealth if we do not pour ourselves out in ministries of mercy at home and missions among the unreached peoples. We are very wealthy in America. All the money needed to send and support an army of self-sacrificing, joy-spreading ambassadors is already in the church. But we are not giving it.

In 1916, Protestants were giving 2.9% of their incomes to their churches. In 1933, the depth of the Great Depression, it was 3.2%. In 1955, just after affluence began spreading through our culture, it was still 3.2%. By 2000, when Americans were over 450% richer, after taxes and inflation, than in the Great Depression, Protestants were giving 2.6% of their incomes to their churches. [21]

Moreover, "If members of historically Christian churches in the United States were giving an average of 10% in 2000, there would have been an additional $139 billion a year going through church channels."[22] Now add to that the really shocking fact that of the money given to the church, less than 6% goes to foreign missions, and of that amount, about 1% goes to fund breakthroughs to unreached peoples.[23] This is not to say we should pull back on any front. The point is, there is plenty for all the breakthroughs if we live to show that Christ is our Treasure.

WE WILL NOT KNOW HIM FULLY OUTSIDE HIS MISSION

For its own soul the church needs to be involved in missions. We will not know God in his full majesty until we know him moving triumphantly among the nations. We will not admire and praise him as we ought until we see him gathering a company of worshipers for himself from every people group on earth—including all the Muslim and Hindu and Buddhist peoples. Nothing enlarges our vision of God's triumphant grace like the scope of his saving work in history. What a story it is! "I will remember the deeds of the LORD; yes, I will remember your wonders of old. I will ponder all your work, and meditate on your mighty deeds" (Psalm 77:11-12). "Praise him for his mighty deeds; praise him according to his excellent greatness!" (Psalm 150:2). "Praise the Lord, all you Gentiles, and let all the peoples extol him" (Romans 15:11, quoting Psalm 117:1).

WHAT IS OUR SITUATION IN THE WORLD TODAY?

The challenges of world evangelization are still very great. We are in a better position to know the scope and nature of the task than ever before. Patrick Johnstone writes, "For the first time in history we have a reasonably complete listing of the world's peoples and the extent to which they have been evangelized."[24] There are various groups that do research to help the church know what people groups around the world have been embraced by a Christian church or mission agency.[25] Johnstone's book gives a good summary of the situation at the turn of our century.[26]

One way to describe the situation is to say that about 1.2–1.4 billion people have never had a chance to hear the Gospel;[27] that is, they live in cultures where the preaching of the Gospel in understandable ways is not accessible. Other analysts estimate the number of unevangelized somewhat higher. For example, the "Annual Statistical Table on Global Mission 2002" by David Barrett and Todd Johnson reports that there are 1,645,685,000 unevangelized people in the world. That means 26.5 percent of the world's population live in people groups that do not have indigenous evangelizing churches.[28] About 95 percent of these live in what has been called the 10/40 window (between latitudes 10 and 40 degrees north of the equator and between the Atlantic and the Pacific Oceans). This is the great challenge of our day.

Johnstone puts it in hopeful historical perspective:

> Stepping back we see a remarkable pattern emerging of the 200 years growth [of the church] as it gathered momentum—1700s the North Atlantic, 1800s the Pacific, 1960s Africa, 1970s Latin America, 1980s East Asia, 1990s Eurasia. This one and a half times encirclement of the globe now leaves us with the challenge of the 10/40 Window area. Central and South Asia and the Middle East are the remaining major areas of challenge. Where will the breakthroughs of the . . . first decade of the . . . [new] millennium come? Will it be among Muslims, Hindus or Buddhists? These are the final unpenetrated bastions of the enemy's hold on the souls of men. The rising tide of the gospel is lapping ever higher round this area, and we are even having foretastes of what that breakthrough might mean. Would that I had the space and the freedom to tell of amazing things going on in these seemingly impenetrable ideological fortresses.[29]

GOD ISSUES A CALL TO THIS GENERATION: LISTEN!

There is a call on this generation to obey the risen Christ and make disciples of all the unreached peoples of the world. I am praying that God will raise up hundreds of thousands of young people and "finishers" (people finishing one career and ready to pursue a second in Christian ministry). I pray that this divine call will rise in your heart with joy and not guilt. I pray that it will be confirmed with the necessary gifts, and a compelling desire, and the confirmation of your church, and the tokens of providence. Fan into flame every flicker of desire by reading biographies, and meditating on Scripture, and studying the unreached peoples, and praying for passion, and conversing with mission veterans. Don't run from the call. Pursue it.

Let your mind dwell on the lostness of perishing individuals, but also on whole people groups that do not have any access to the Gospel. This was Paul's great ambition: "to preach the gospel, not where Christ has already been named" (Romans 15:20). There will always be unconverted people to win where the church is already established. That is not the unique task of frontier missions. Frontier missions does what Paul aimed to do: Plant the church where there is now no possibility of ministry. This is the great need of the hour, not only for missionaries who go to serve the established church in other countries (which is a great need, especially in leadership development), but also for missionaries who go to peoples and places where there *is* no church to serve.

THE DAY OF MISSIONS IS NOT OVER

Don't think the days of foreign missionaries are over, as if nationals can finish the work. There are hundreds of peoples and millions of people where there are no Christian nationals to do same-culture evangelism. A culture must be crossed. To be sure, it may be crossed by a non-Westerner, since God is growing his church faster in the non-Western world.[30] That would be wonderful. I have no desire to limit the joy of love. Besides, it may be that highly trained but tentative Western specialists will not be as fruitful as simpler, bold missionaries. Regarding missions to Muslims Patrick Johnstone says, "Often the best missionaries are the ones who have studied little more than the basics of Islamics but have a passion for sharing Christ. In their boldness for Jesus, they plunge into witnessing to Muslims, where an Islamist would fear to go."[31] But make no mistake. A culture will have to be crossed, and that's what missions is. Missions, not same-culture evangelism by nationals, will finish the Great Commission.

So "pray earnestly to the Lord of the harvest to send out laborers into his harvest" (Matthew 9:38), and ask him if you should be one. Expect this prayer to change you. When Jesus told his disciples to pray it, the next thing that happened was that he appointed twelve to be his apostles and sent them out. Pray for harvesters, and you may become one. God often wakens desire, and gives gifts, and opens doors when we are praying and pondering real possibilities and real needs. Get a copy of the amazing world prayer guide called *Operation World*, and pray and read and ponder your way through the nations day by day.[32] Think about the people in places like

- *Libya* with its six million people and perhaps ten indigenous believers.
- *Bhutan*, a hermit Buddhist kingdom in the Himalayas, cut off from Christian witness for millennia with only a handful of indigenous believers among its two and a half million people.
- *The Maldives*, off the southwest coast of India, and one of the most closed countries on earth.
- *North Korea*, "a pariah nation gradually starving to death under its crazed Communist leadership,"[33] with no open witness or church life for fifty years.
- *Saudi Arabia*, the headquarters of Islam where Saudi believers, if found, are executed.
- *India*, perhaps the greatest challenge of all, with its vast Ganges plains that contain "the greatest concentration of unevangelized people in the world. For instance, the number of people in Uttar Pradesh in North India is about 180,000,000 and the Christian percentage is 0.1% and falling."[34]
- *Turkey*, the secular, mainly Muslim state with an ongoing Christian witness in only fifteen of its 100 provinces.

PONDER THE AMNESTY OFFERED TO THE NATIONS. TAKE A RETREAT

The point of that fragmentary list is to simply illustrate whole populations living in rebellion against the true God and cut off from the only One who can reconcile them to their Maker. This means destruction for the unbelieving and dishonor to Christ. He owns this world, and the allegiance of every person is his right. Every soul and every state is his. Abraham Kuyper put it memorably: "There is not a square inch in the whole domain of our human existence over which Christ, who is Sovereign over all, does not cry: 'Mine!'"[35] Christ has come into this mutinous world, which he made for his own glory, and paid for an amnesty with his own blood. Everyone who lays down the weaponry of unbelief will be absolved from all crimes against the Sovereign of the universe. By faith alone enemies will become happy subjects of an everlasting kingdom of justice and joy. Advancing this cause with Christ is worth your life.

No, you don't have to be a missionary to admire and advance the great purposes of God to be known and praised and enjoyed among all peoples. But if you want to be most fully satisfied with God as he triumphs in the history of redemption, you can't go on with business as usual—doing your work, making your money, giving your tithe, eating, sleeping, playing, and going to church. Instead you need to stop and go away for a few days with a Bible and notepad; and pray and think about how your particular time and place in life fits into the great purpose of God to make the nations glad in him. How will you join the great global purpose of God expressed in Psalm 67:4, "Let the nations be glad and sing for joy"?

THE MEANING OF YOUR DISCONTENT

Many of you should stay where you are in your present job, and simply ponder how you can fit your particular skills and relationships and resources more strategically into the global purpose of your heavenly Father. But for others reading this book, it is going to be different. Many of you are simply not satisfied with what you are doing. As J. Campbell White said, the output of your lives is not satisfying your deepest spiritual ambitions. We must be careful here. Every job has its discouragements and its seasons of darkness. We must not interpret such experiences automatically as a call to leave our post.

But if the discontent with your present situation is deep, recurrent, and lasting, and if that discontent grows in Bible-saturated soil, God may be calling you to a new work. If, in your discontent, you long to be holy, to walk pleasing to the Lord, and to magnify Christ with your one, brief life, then God may indeed be loosening your roots in order to transplant you to a place and a ministry where the deep spiritual ambitions of your soul can be satisfied. It is true that God can be known and enjoyed in every legitimate vocation; but when he deploys you from one place to the next, he offers fresh and deeper drinking at the fountain of his fellowship. God seldom calls us to an easier life, but always calls us to know more of him and drink more deeply of his sustaining grace.

SHOULD I GO ON BEING A PASTOR?

I try to take stock of my own ministry in this way. Every year at our church we have a "Missions Week." I preach on missions; we have guest speakers. The challenge is given. People move toward missions, make commitments, and join the pre-missions nurture program. And every year I reexamine my life as a pastor at this church. I look at what I am doing in the light of God's global purpose, and in view of the incredible spiritual darkness and misery of the unreached peoples of this earth. I ask myself, Is this the most strategic investment of my life for the sake of God's purpose to make the nations glad in him? I ask my wife, "Noël, are you sensing any tugs to move closer to the front lines of the unreached peoples?"

Our church mission statement puts the world "spread" in

the dominant position: "We exist to *spread* a passion for God's supremacy in all things for the joy of all peoples through Jesus Christ." So I ask, Am I fulfilling this mission best in the role I now have? When the Lord calls me to give an account of my ministry in the last day, will I be able to say, "Lord, I stayed at Bethlehem because I believed I could be most instrumental there in accomplishing your purpose to make a name for yourself among the nations, and to gather your sheep from all the peoples of the earth"? When I can no longer say yes to that question, then my leadership here will be finished.

AND YOU?

And so it is with many of you. Big issues are in the offing. May God help you. May God free you. May God give you a fresh, Christ-exalting vision for your life—whether you go to an unreached people or stay firmly and fruitfully at your present post. May your vision get its meaning from God's great purpose to make the nations glad in him. May the cross of Christ be your only boast, and may you say, with sweet confidence, to live is Christ, and to die is gain.

NOTES

1 For more on Adoniram Judson, see John Piper, *Filling Up the Afflictions of Christ: The Cost of Bringing the Gospel to the Nations in the Lives of William Tyndale, Adoniram Judson, and John Paton*, The Swans Are Not Silent (Wheaton, Ill.: Crossway Books, 2009).

2 Courtney Anderson, *To the Golden Shore: The Life of Adoniram Judson* (Grand Rapids, Mich.: Zondervan, 1956), 14.

3 Deism was "the belief, based solely on reason, in a God who created the universe and then abandoned it, assuming no control over life, exerting no influence on natural phenomena, and giving no supernatural revelation," *The American Heritage Dictionary* (http://www.bartleby.com/61/44/D0104400.html, accessed 4-3-03).

4 Anderson, *To the Golden Shore*, 41.

5 Ibid., 42.

6 Ibid., 44. The source of this story is oral reports from family members recorded in Francis Wayland, *A Memoir of the Life and Labors of the Rev. Adoniram Judson, D. D.*, Vol. 1 (Boston: Phillips, Sampson, and Co., 1854), 24-25.

7 Anderson, *To the Golden Shore*, 45.

8 Ibid., 83.

9 *The Bethlehem Institute Affirmation of Faith* can be read in its entirety at http://desiringgod.org/library/what_we_believe/tbi_affirmation.html.

10 B. B. Warfield, *The Person and Work of Christ* (Philadelphia: Presbyterian & Reformed, 1950), 574. I found this quoted in Timothy J. Keller's book, *Ministries of Mercy: The Call of the Jericho Road* (Phillipsburg, N. J.: Presbyterian & Reformed, 1997), 65. I wish every one of my readers would read this book.

11 Kenneth Scott Latourette, *These Sought a Country* (New York: Harper and Brothers, 1950), 46.

12 John R. Mott, *Five Decades and a Forward View* (New York: Harper and Brothers, 1939), 8.

13 David Howard, "Student Power in Missions," in *Perspectives on the World Christian Movement: A Reader*, 2nd edition, eds. Ralph D. Winter and Steven C. Hawthorne (Pasadena, Ca.: William Carey Library, 1999), 283. Most of the facts I have recorded here about the SVM come from this article.

14 Ruth Rouse and Stephen C. Neill, *A History of the Ecumenical Movement, 1517-1948* (Philadelphia: Westminster, 1967), 328.

15 J. Campbell White, "The Layman's Missionary Movement," in Ralph D. Winter and Steven C. Hawthorne, eds., *Perspectives on the World Christian Movement: A Reader*, 1st edition (Pasadena, Ca.: William Carey Library, 1981), 222.

16 Ibid., 223.

17 Ibid., 224.

18 Ibid., 225.

19 Ibid., 224.

20 Ibid., 225.

21 http://www.emptytomb.org/research.html [accessed 3-28-03].

22 http://www.emptytomb.org/Chapter6hlites.html [accessed 3-28-03].

23 http://www.missionfrontiers.org/newslinks/statewe.htm [accessed 3-28-03].

24 Patrick Johnstone, *The Church Is Bigger Than You Think* (Ross-shire, England: Christian Focus, 1998), 229.

25 See, for example, http://www.ad2000.org/peoples/jpllist.pdf; http://www.joshuaproject.net/; http://www.calebproject.org/maps.htm

26 Johnstone, *The Church Is Bigger Than You Think*, 225-230.

27 Ibid., 215. Johnstone is more optimistic than Barrett in his numbers: About 20% of the world's population are unevangelized; 47% are non-Christians living where they are likely to be evangelized; and 33% are professing Christians.

28 David B. Barrett and Todd M. Johnson, "Annual Statistical Table on Global Mission 2002," *International Bulletin of Missionary Research* 26 (January 2002): 22-23.

29 Johnstone, *The Church Is Bigger Than You Think*, 115-116.

30 This growth in the twentieth century is documented by Philip Jenkins, *The New Christendom* (Oxford: Oxford University Press, 2002).

> Over the past century . . . the center of gravity in the Christian world has shifted inexorably southward to Africa, Asia, and Latin America. Already today the largest Christian communities on the planet are to be found in Africa and Latin America. If we want to visualize a 'typical' contemporary Christian, we should think of a woman living in a village in Nigeria or in a Brazilian favela. As Kenyan scholar John Mbiti has observed, "the centers of the church's universality [are] no longer in Geneva, Rome, Athens, Paris, London, New York, but in Kinshasa, Buenos Aires, Addis Ababa and Manila. Whatever Europeans or North Americans may believe, Christianity is doing very well indeed in the global South—not just surviving, but expanding." (p. 2)

31 Johnstone, *The Church Is Bigger Than You Think*, 273.

32 Patrick Johnstone and Jason Mandryk, *Operation World: When We Pray God Works* (Waynesboro, Ga.: Paternoster USA, 2001). See the online version at http://www.operationworld.org.

33 Ibid., 222.

34 Ibid., 223.

35 Abraham Kuyper, "Sphere Sovereignty," in Abraham Kuyper, *A Centennial Reader*, ed. James D. Bratt (Grand Rapids, Mich.: Eerdmans, 1998), 488.

CHAPTER 10
MY PRAYER—LET NONE SAY IN THE END, "I'VE WASTED IT"

*Y*our steadfast love, O Lord, is better than life. You have told us this in many ways. With these very words you have said it through the mouth of your servant David: "Because your steadfast love is better than life, my lips will praise you." You have said it in the words of your apostle Paul, when he cried out in prison, "My desire is to depart and be with Christ, for that is far better." O Lord, how much better you are than life! Does your apostle Paul not use strong language! Not just "better," but "far better." You are so much better than life that your apostle says death is gain. "To live is Christ, and to die is gain." To lose everything this world can offer and be left with you alone is gain.

Why, O Lord, is your love better than life? Surely David gives us the answer in the way he speaks. He does not say, "Because your steadfast love is better than life, my lips will praise *your love*." What does he say? He says that he will praise *you*, not your love. "Because your steadfast love is better than life, my lips will praise *you*." Is this not because the most loving thing about your love is that it brings us home to you—with eyes and hearts and minds able to see the riches of your glory? With all your wrath removed, and all our sin forgiven, lest anything prevent the pleasure of your presence. Is this not what divine love is—the will and work of God, to give us undeserving sinners everlasting joy in God? What else could love be, if it would be infinite! What greater prize might we be given than yourself, if we are loved!

O God, you know I tremble now for fear that many of the ones who call you Lord have made *themselves* the prize and glory of your grace. How many, Lord, have made your love a witness to *their* worth! Is then their joy a resting in *your* worth or in their own? So many decades have gone by in which the constant message from the world, and even from some ministers, is this: that love means making much of man. And so when men, with this assurance, ponder what *your* love might mean, they say the same: God's love means making much of man. For proof they ask: Don't you feel loved when someone calls attention to your worth?

I answer: Once I did. When life was better than the Lord, and not the other way around. There was a time love felt like this— when I could not conceive of any joy greater than the honor of my name. When I was so absorbed in me that it was inconceivable for joy to rise by my admiring rather than my being admired. Oh, yes, I've known what it is like to call the praise of men an act of love and justify this craving with the readiness to give the same. How satisfying it does seem—this love among ourselves of mutual admiration!

But now (thanks to your mighty grace!) I see it is an imitation. It has its roots in Eden long ago. The great destroyer of our love and joy said to our mother, Eve, "God knows that when you eat of it, your eyes will be opened, and you will be like God." Like God! She should have said, "I am like God already." She should have seen the trick. But she did not, and oh, how many do not see it yet today! She was indeed like God! You made her so—your very image-bearer. Her calling and her high design was this: to image forth her Maker's majesty, and with her joy and trust, make much of you. But then the evil thought was sown: "I could be like him in another way. I could be one whose majesty is seen, and love might be defined as making much of me."

And so it came into the world, this great inversion we call sin. And love was made to stand now on its head. I grieve, Lord, just to put it into words, but here it is with shame: Your love no longer means that you do what you must do to make yourself our joy. It has come to mean that you do what you must do so we can feel our worth. It was a sad exchange. And doubly so: Not only did it rob our souls of that one joy that you designed to satisfy us for eternity, but worse, it robbed you of your honored place as Treasure of our lives.

And everything you've done since that dark day in Eden is designed to set things right. Oh, what a history of deeds and revelations you have wrought to make yourself the center of our joy and take back for yourself the place of honor in the world—to be the One your people treasure more than life. How many ways you said and showed, "I made you for my glory. I made you for my praise. I made you for my honor and my name." And, lest we miss the point, you added: "In my presence there is fullness of joy; at my right hand are pleasures forevermore. Delight yourself in me! Be glad in me and leap for joy; I am your sure and great Reward! Come taste, and even now rejoice with joy unspeakable and full of glory."

Oh, what a grand design! To make our joy the echo of your excellence. To make our pleasure proof that you now hold the place of Treasure in our lives. To make the gladness of our souls the essence of our worship, and the mirror of your worth. To make yourself most glorified in us, O God, when we are satisfied in you. How could I, Lord, have ever been so blind to think that being loved by you means making much of me and not yourself? How could I put my eye to some great telescope, designed to make me glad with visions of the galaxies, and notice in the glass a dim reflection of my face and say, "Now I am happy, I am loved"? How could I stand before the setting sun, between the mountain range and the vastness of the sea, and think that everlasting joy should come from making much of me?

No, Father, love is this: At great expense you made yourself my glory and my boast. The cost was infinite by which you made yourself the Treasure of my life. You sent your Son, the blazing center of your beauty and your love. You gave him up to mockery, betrayal, thorns, the whip, the rod, the fists, the nails, the shame, and death. For what? To swallow up your wrath, and satisfy your righteousness, and bury all my sins as far as east is from the west and in the deepest sea, so that I might come home and see the galaxy. This is your love, O God, not to make much of me, but do whatever must be done so that I waken to the joy of making much of you through all eternity.

How then shall Christ not be my only boast! Not only that he bought yourself for me, O God, but is himself your perfect image and the blazing center of your radiance. What do I have that does not come from him? What gift of life or breath? What promise ever made did not receive its Yes in him? What one sweet thing—or hard thing you will soon make sweet—did I receive except that it was purchased by his blood? Not one thing I deserve, but hell. Yet everything is mine in him, and by his sacrifice alone. O God, forbid that I should ever boast save in the cross of Christ, my Lord.

And now shall we who treasure Christ and know your love is better far than life lay up, like all the world, our treasures on this earth? Would not we hear you say, as you once said, "Fool, will not this same night your soul be taken back? And then whose will these barns of bounty be?" Forbid, O Lord, that while the world is filled with need we would sit down and say, "Soul, you have

ample goods laid up for many years; relax, eat, drink, be merry."
A terrible reversal awaits such lovelessness. "Woe to you who are
rich, for you have received your consolation." We tremble at the
words you spoke once to the heartless rich: "Remember in your
lifetime you received good things, and that poor man, beside your
door, received the pain; but now the great reversal comes, and he
has comfort here, while you lie there in anguish."

O God, such riches are a wasted life. Protect us, Lord. Grant
us to hear and heed another call: "Lay up your treasure not on
earth, but in the place where moth and thief will never come.
Make treasures for yourself that cannot fail." But then we ask,
"What treasures, Lord?" We see you smile. "I am your Treasure
and your great Reward. I am your food, your drink, your festal
garments and your everlasting gain. I am your life and your all-
satisfying Joy."

Yes, Lord. That is enough. But we would ask, How shall we
lay this treasure up? Is it not laid there by your grace alone and
bought now once for all by Jesus' blood? How shall we make
this life—this brief and only life that we now live—a laying up
of treasure there in heaven? To answer this, you know, O God,
that I have written this small book. And I have looked not to
myself or listened to some voice. But I have tried to probe your
written Word and say what you have said. That is my only claim
to truth—that I have echoed what you wrote.

The answer is that in this life we may begin to treasure Christ,
and here gain, as it were, an aptitude for joy in him. A greater
weight of glory waits to be enjoyed for those who grow in love
to Christ. And what is love to Christ? It is the cherishing of all
you are for us in him. It is the treasuring of his perfection over
all the treasures of the world. It is delighting in his fellowship
beyond all family and friends. It is embracing all his promises
that there will be more pleasure in his presence than from all the
lying promises of sin. It is a gladness in the present taste of glory

and the hope of future fullness when we see him face to face. It is a quiet peace along the path he chooses for us with its pain. It is a being satisfied that nothing comes to us in vain.

There is a quiet kind of joy, O Lord, that Jesus did both save us from our sin and show us how to love. His life, as you have said, was both a purchase and a path. He died for us, and now calls us to die with him. He took our poverty upon himself that we, in him, might have the riches of his heaven, and he calls us now to use our riches for the poor. He did not count equality with you a thing to grasp, but made himself of no account and crossed an endless chasm between heaven and earth, so we might see what frontier missions means and join him in the final task. Is not this, then, the way we lay up treasure in your house—to give our money and ourselves to make as many rich with God forever as we can?

A quiet kind of joy, I say, because of so much suffering. I cannot rise above the great apostle Paul who called his life a daily death and put it in a paradox: "sorrowful, yet always rejoicing; poor, yet making many rich; having nothing, yet possessing everything." O Father, grant your church to love your glory more than gold—to cease her love affair with comfort and security. Grant that we seek the kingdom first and let the other things come as you will. Grant that we move toward need and not toward ease. Grant that the firm finality of our security in Christ free us to risk our homes and health and money on the earth. Help us to see that if we try to guard our wealth, instead of using it to show it's not our god, then we will waste our lives, however we succeed.

Dear Lord, I tremble now to pray for readers what I barely feel myself. But I have tasted what our life might be if I, and they, could walk along the ever-present edge of death, and smile with utter confidence that if we fell, or possibly were pushed, it would be gain. Oh, what abandon, what great liberty, what invincible resolve to love would be our portion if we walked this way! What readiness to suffer for the glory of Christ! What eagerness to show the poor that we would gladly spend and be spent to make them glad in God for all eternity! What lowliness and meekness and freedom from the need for praise and pay! All things are ours in Christ—the world, life, death, the present, the future. All are ours, and we are Christ's. And none of it deserved.

And so, dear Lord, I dare to pray that everything I've written in this book, if it be true, explode with fear-defeating joy in Jesus Christ. Let every wavering heart remember this: You promised, "I will never leave you nor forsake you." So may we say with death-defying confidence, "The Lord is my helper; I will not fear; what can man do to me?"

Forbid that any, Lord, who read these words would have to say someday, "I've wasted it." But grant, by your almighty Spirit and your piercing Word, that we who name Christ as the Lord would treasure him above our lives, and feel, deep in our souls, that Christ is life and death is gain. And so may we display his worth for all to see. And by our prizing him may he be praised in all the world. May he be magnified in life and death. May every neighborhood and nation see how joy in Jesus frees his people from the power of greed and fear.

Let love flow from your saints, and may it, Lord, be this: that even if it costs our lives, the people will be glad in God. "Let the peoples praise you, O God; let all the peoples praise you! Let the nations be glad and sing for joy." Take your honored place, O Christ, as the all-satisfying Treasure of the world. With trembling hands before the throne of God, and utterly dependent on your grace, we lift our voice and make this solemn vow: As God lives, and is all I ever need, I will not waste my life . . .

through Jesus Christ, Amen.

❄ desiring God

If you would like to further explore the vision of God and life presented in this book, we at Desiring God would love to serve you. We have hundreds of resources to help you grow in your passion for Jesus Christ and help you spread that passion to others. At our website, desiringGod.org, you'll find almost everything John Piper has written and preached, including more than thirty books. We've made over twenty-five years of his sermons available free online for you to read, listen to, download, and in some cases watch.

In addition, you can access hundreds of articles, listen to our daily internet radio program, find out where John Piper is speaking, learn about our conferences, discover our God-centered children's curricula, and browse our online store. John Piper receives no royalties from the books he writes and no compensation from Desiring God. The funds are all reinvested into our gospel-spreading efforts. DG also has a whatever-you-can-afford policy, designed for individuals with limited discretionary funds. If you'd like more information about this policy, please contact us at the address or phone number below. We exist to help you treasure Jesus Christ and his gospel above all things because he is most glorified in you when you are most satisfied in him. Let us know how we can serve you!

Desiring God
Post Office Box 2901
Minneapolis, Minnesota 55402

888.346.4700
mail@desiringGod.org
www.desiringGod.org